SIR GAWAIN
AND THE GRENE GOME

Gawain and the Grene Knight

SIR GAWAIN

AND THE GRENE GOME

A regularized text
prepared and introduced by
R. T. JONES
Senior Lecturer in English,
University of York

BARNES & NOBLE, INC.
NEW YORK
Publishers & Booksellers since 1873

ISBN 389 04497 0

This regularized text first published by University of Natal
Press 1962
This edition with new matter © R. T. Jones 1972
First published 1972

First published in the United States by
Barnes & Noble, New York 1003
Printed in Great Britain

INTRODUCTION

1. THE POEM

> *Nere slain with the slete he sleped in his irnes*
> *Mo nightes then innowe in naked rokkes,*
> *There as claterande fro the crest the colde borne rennes*
> *And henged high over his hed in hard iisse-ikkles.*

The phrase *in his irnes* will not permit us to think of *this* knight-errant merely as a fit subject for technicolor, with armour that might as well be made of tinsel so long as it can dazzle the eyes of fair maidens. In the physical discomfort of reading the phrase, and momentarily enduring as we must the weight, the hardness and above all the coldness of iron, we are obliged to recognize an experience lived through in an awakened imagination. We can no more agree or disagree with it that we can with last Friday's thunderstorm; and whether we like it or not it has become, once we have read it, a part of our own experience that we must come to terms with and find a place for in the totality of our experience.

A summary of the story might contain the statement: "The next morning, the lady again visited Gawain in his bedroom." No doubt some such statement occurred, too, in one of the poem's "sources" (for hardly a single material incident in the poem, as far as I can see, is original). But what the poet says is:

> *Ho comes withinne the chamber dore and closes hit hir after,*
> *Waives up a window, and on the wighe calles . . .*

It is no fairy tale bedroom that needs to have a window opened; nor is it a fairy-tale damsel who recognizes the stuffiness of the room as soon as she enters it. Such apparent trivialities as these are our guarantee that this poet's imagination has its roots in an intense awareness of reality, not in wishes or theories: that the poem is neither make-believe nor propaganda.

In the lines I quoted first, the cold is felt through the conjunction of sound and sense in

> *There as claterande fro the crest the cold borne rennes.*

We know, in fact, that ice is forming in this water before we are told of it in the next line (with its striking vision of icicles suspended like so many swords of Damocles over the sleeping Gawain, prefiguring the temptations in which Nature in another guise threatens the embodiment of Christian civilization).

1

But this, it may be objected, is merely onomatopoeia—a device, a technique, easily acquired by an alliterating poet and guaranteeing nothing. Let us consider, then, the line

There thre thro at a thrich thrat him at ones.

The line in its context is somehow full of the snapping of dogs. But how? No sound in the line imitates the sound of snapping jaws. This, then, is not onomatopoeia. But one cannot speak the line, with its profusion of *th* sounds, without becoming intensely aware of teeth—one's own teeth. This sequence of words could only have occurred to someone whose imagination was compelling him to participate in (not merely to observe or to listen to) the snapping of dogs.

But while the poem compels us to share the experience it describes (any man who is not disturbed by the physical presence of Gawain's temptress might as well turn to Henry Miller without further waste of time), it is far from being, in its total effect, "sensational". I may as well return to the lines quoted at the beginning of this Introduction, and refer to the phrase *Mo nightes then innowe.* The wry fellow-feeling implicit in this understatement is characteristic of that voice that becomes audible and familiar to us when, after the first hundred lines or so, the strangeness of the poem's vocabulary ceases to obscure its wholly English rhythms and intonations. The voice we hear speaking these words, though far from unsympathetic, is quite unsensational, disenchanted; detached, though never indifferent. It is capable of ironical inflections*—of reducing the tears of Gawain's admirers in Camelot to

Wel much was the warme water that waltered of ighen.

The sanity of this voice is our guide in strange lands, and it never falters.

Clearly we should not find it necessary or useful to look for a "meaning" in the poem as a whole, if we were not convinced by its parts of the validity of the experience it communicates. To find its meaning is, in fact, to find some way of assimilating into the totality of our experience (of life and literature together) the sum of what we have gone through in reading the poem. There is no simple and sufficient formula that can relieve the reader of the necessity of performing this task for himself. Nor has even the most complex interpretation that I have yet devised commanded that general assent that would assure me that I had achieved the right

---

*The voice of this narrator has affinities with that of Marlow in Conrad's *Heart of Darkness*, a work which might, in several respects, be usefully compared with *Sir Gawain*.

2

reading of the poem. The tentative interpretation that follows, then, is offered as a hypothesis that has served some readers, and may serve others, as a point of departure: the authoritative critical analysis of the poem has yet to be written.

The poem is about the testing of Sir Gawain as the representative of the ideal of Christian chivalry and "cortaisie", the ideal embodied imaginatively in mediaeval treatments of the legends of King Arthur and his knights and of a past that was generally regarded as the good old days—the standard by which the decay of morals and manners was measured.

The test begins with an encounter with a strange outsider, who rides into Arthur's court in the middle of the Christmas festivities and requests, by way of a Christmas game, that one of the knights should strike him a blow with his great axe, the blow to be returned after one year. The strangest thing about him, apart from the fact that he wants his head cut off, is that he is green. Even his long hair and his beard like a bush (both cut at elbow-level, so that the "bush" encloses him down to the waist) are green; and besides the axe he carries a branch of holly *that is grattest in grene when greves are bare*. Scholars do not like us to think of him as a nature god, so we must say warily that he looks remarkably like Jack-in-the-green in several village festivals (and the garland-wearer in the Castleton garland ceremony); that he seems to have something to do with vegetation; that he speaks as one with authority; that he requires to have his head cut off; and that when Gawain (having done him that service) asks him where he is to be found at the end of the year, he gives no address but says in effect, "If you seek me you will never fail to find me".

Such is the being who conducts the examination. But how can anybody evaluate one civilization without assuming the values of another? In the poem this problem is triumphantly surmounted. The tests there applied have a general validity, since they correspond to those to which every civilization, whatever its explicit values, is subjected by the natural world: tests of the individual's ability to survive in a hostile and unfamiliar environment and of his fidelity to an agreement; that is, tests of the civilization's fostering both of individual resourcefulness and of social coherence.

Gawain survives. In a sense he owes his survival to his own merit; but it is also by an act of grace that the green man reduces the beheading stroke that he is entitled to give to a mere scratch in the neck with the great axe.

I have asserted (leaving verification to the reader) the importance

3

of the issues with which the poem is concerned. I must also assert, for there is no room for demonstration, the delicacy and precision with which these issues are explored. Near the end of his journey Gawain rests at a northern castle, and agrees to the joking suggestion of his host (later identified as the green man in another guise) that they should exchange at the end of the day all that they have won during the day. The host goes out hunting, while Gawain stays in bed where he is entertained and tempted by the lady of the castle. Each evening the lord of the castle gives Gawain what he has caught and gets in exchange the kisses Gawain has had from the lady. On the last day Gawain breaks his agreement by accepting from the lady, and concealing from her husband, a green girdle which, she has told him, will save his life. The contrast, emphasized by abrupt changes of scene, between hunting field and bedroom is part of the whole delicately drawn contrast between the court of Arthur, *so joly of his joifnes, and sumwhat childgered*, where *al was this fair folk in her first age*, and the northern court, where the lord is

> *A huge hathel for the nones, and of high elde;*
> *Brode, bright was his berde, and al bever-hued,*
> *Sturn, stif on the strithe on stalworth shankes,*
> *Felle face as the fire, and fre of his speche;*

and the company expects Gawain to teach it all about *luf-talking*. The contrast is not a matter of extremes; the northern court, though not dedicated to Christian chivalry and "cortaisie", has a chapel and chaplains, and its lord, for all his customary bluntness, shows himself capable of *Frenkish fare* when he says it was good of Gawain to *enbelise his burgh with his bele chere*. Conversely, the bravery of Arthur's knights is not in question (they can hardly be blamed for their hesitancy when confronted by a green man), but their characteristic pursuits are considerably less vigorous than those of the northern court. Arthur waits for a marvel to enliven the Christmas feasts; the other lord makes his own marvels. All this, and much more, is involved in the poem's final judgement.

So Mary's knight wins a green girdle. This event has at least three meanings: what the green man means by the gift, what Gawain takes it to mean, and what Arthur's court makes of it. Perhaps, too, even after the explicit *dénouement*, we may not be entirely convinced that we know what the lady meant by the gift. The meaning of the poem is contained in the interaction of all these.

But at the same time the meaning of the poem is in the very texture of the poetry, the unwavering sureness and control with which the poet's voice guides us—for all our uncertainties about particular words—through the intricacies of the narrative. It is in the achieved directness and simplicity of a highly sophisticated mind in complete command of its material.

These are unsupported assertions. The reader who wishes to challenge them will have to read the poem in order to do so. This has been my object in these introductory pages.

2. CRITICAL WORKS

A great deal has been written about *Sir Gawain,* but most of it has been at best peripheral to the meaning of the poem. There have been attempts to identify the "Green Knight" as a historical personage, and to locate the Green Chapel geographically. There have been investigations of the literary sources of the poem, which have established that there is nothing new in it, except the whole poem. The anonymity of the author has provoked attempts to identify him, and to establish that he also wrote the other poems in the same dialect contained in the same manuscript, though so far little investigation of why it should matter.

The first critical work of any importance on the poem, and still, I think, the best, is an essay by John Speirs, which first appeared in *Scrutiny,* Vol. XVI, No. 4 (1949), pp. 274–300, and ·was later revised and included in his *Medieval English Poetry: The Non-Chaucerian Tradition* (Faber & Faber, 1957). It was this essay that first drew attention to the poem as an important work of art.

It is not difficult to detect flaws in some of the branches of Mr Speirs' argument, but one's sense of the truth and importance of the whole is likely to be strengthened by a perusal of some of the published attacks on it. The most respectable of these are Charles Moorman's "Myth and Medieval Literature: *Sir Gawain and the Green Knight"* in *Mediaeval Studies,* Vol. XVIII (1956), pp. 158–172, and C. S. Lewis's "The Anthropological Approach" in *English and Medieval Studies Presented to J. R. R. Tolkien* on the Occasion of his Seventieth Birthday,* ed. Norman Davis and C. L. Wrenn (Allen & Unwin, 1962). But in spite of the controversy it has provoked, the essay has only recently begun to receive the attention it deserves. For the controversy has centred on the background information that Mr Speirs found it necessary to offer, concerning the significance of the Green Man in relation to traditional dances and festivities, fertility cults and the Old Religion generally; so that it has distracted attention from what is of more central importance in the essay: its demonstration of the poetic quality—the Shakespearean quality, in

---

*Mr Speirs had written unkindly of Professor Tolkien's edition of the poem.

fact—of the language of the poem. The disputes about the sources of the poem were, finally, an evasion of the impact of the poem, and of Mr Speirs' demonstration of its force.

Fifteen years after he had thus rocked the goldfish bowl of medieval scholarship, A. C. Spearing's *Criticism and Medieval Poetry* (Arnold, 1964) cautiously set out to suggest that medieval poetry could be read with critical attention. The chapter on *Sir Gawain* contains some illuminating analysis.

Another valuable contribution to the understanding of the poem —this time an entire book on it—is J. A. Burrow's *A Reading of Sir Gawain and the Green Knight* (Routledge & Kegan Paul, 1965). This works through the poem step by step, makes some interesting critical observations, and usefully defines a number of problems in interpretation. Mr Burrow recognizes that the poem is *about* something—"truth" in the sense of loyalty—and that its theme is to be taken seriously. Besides being often directly helpful, this book discusses the poem in sufficient detail for the reader to be able to locate precisely his disagreements with the author, and thus to formulate his own account of the poem.

Mr Spearing returns to the field, more boldly than before, with *The Gawain-Poet, A Critical Study* (Cambridge University Press, 1970). Again there is a good deal of very interesting analysis, offered this time without the embarrassment that characterized his earlier book. Apparently one can now assume that even specialists know something of critical analysis and close reading. Part of Mr Spearing's evidence for the common authorship of the four poems in the manuscript is "the common central image (of man confronted and baffled by a non-human power)"; the reader may well think that what he actually shows in the poems is several *different* images of encounters between man and the non-human, and that the *Gawain*-poet's apprehension of the non-human is very different from that of the *Pearl*-poet. Perhaps this is why this book shows a determined lack of interest in the greenness of the "gome in the grene."

No reader ought to allow himself to be intimidated by the weight of scholarship that tends to interpose itself between him and the poem, or to consider himself unqualified to read it without a great accumulation of knowledge. But neither ought the reader to hesitate to make use of the relevant scholarship when he needs it. He may well find that, on the language and style of the poem, Marie Borroff's *Sir Gawain and the Green Knight: A Stylistic and Metrical Study* (Yale University Press, 1962) is often helpful in its application of the results of philological investigations to the study of the poem. This book is a rare example of thorough scholarship in the service of a responsive appreciation of the poem.

The sources of the story and the literary conventions of allitera-
tive verse can be explored through L. D. Benson's *Art and Tradition
in Sir Gawain and the Green Knight* (Rutgers University Press, 1965),
in which the notes are a useful guide to such further reading as one
might wish to pursue. The author's application of his background
information to a reading of the poem, however, is not always convin-
cing.

Exploring the poem from another direction, one can very profit-
ably turn to a modern dramatist's re-interpretation of the poem. In
The Green Knight (Human & Rousseau, 1962), H. W. D. Manson
transposes what he takes to be the central truth of the poem into
twentieth-century terms, though the setting remains medieval and
much of the dialogue is very close in spirit to the poem. A comparison
of the play with the poem on which it is based is a good approach to
defining the significance of the poem as a whole and the tone of
several of the conversations.

3. THE TEXT

This poem suffers from the disadvantage of having survived
in only one manuscript (known as MS. Nero A. x.). The scribe
wrote neatly, but his spelling is extremely inconsistent. Editors of
Chaucer, having to work from several manuscripts, find it necessary
to adopt a fairly consistent spelling based on a comparison of the
various spellings of their sources; but the editors of *Sir Gawain*
have generally been content to follow the only surviving manuscript
letter for letter.

The two most recent editions of this kind are:
Sir Gawain and the Green Knight, ed. J. R. R. Tolkien and
E. V. Gordon, O.U.P., 1925; Revised Edition, 1967;
Sir Gawain and the Green Knight, ed Sir Israel Gollancz, with
introductory essays by Mabel Day and Mary S. Serjeantson,
O.U.P. for the Early English Text Society, 1940.

I wish at this point to record my indebtedness to both of these editions. The student who is concerned with Middle English as a field
of linguistic study will turn to these editions rather than to mine,
which is intended for the student of English poetry. He will also
make use of the invaluable *Facsimile of MS Cotton Nero A. x.*,
introduced by Sir Israel Gollancz (E.E.T.S., 1923).

The edition by A. C. Cawley, *"Pearl" and "Sir Gawain and the
Green Knight"* (Everyman, 1962), and that by R. A. Waldron, *Sir
Gawain and the Green Knight* (Arnold, 1970), have made some

cautious moves in the direction of normalizing the spelling by modernizing obsolete characters and adapting some others to modern practice, but otherwise they carefully retain all the manuscript's inconsistencies. The second has an interesting and helpful introduction.

A text of the poem is also given in *A Guide to English Literature*, Vol. I (Pelican, 1954). Here an attempt is made to regularize the spelling, but this has not been done systematically and the result is often confusing.

What I have done is to select one of the scribe's spellings of each word, and use that spelling consistently throughout the poem. Even this presented some problems; I have regarded *aventure* and *aunter* as different words, but *quaint* and *coint* merely as different spellings of the same word. Further, I have followed the practice of editors of Chaucer by adjusting to modern usage the *u* and *v*, the *i* and *j*, and the *i* and *y* of the manuscript, where these pairs of letters are interchangeable. Two symbols not used in modern printing have been replaced: one by *th;* the other by *gh, y, g, w* or *s,* and in deciding which to use I have seen no reason to prefer Old English to Modern English as a guide. The manuscript inserts final *e* or omits it without grammatical significance or alteration of sound (as several rhymes show), so I have again chosen the more modern form where both appear in the manuscript.

The result, I hope, is a text that is free of unnecessary difficulties and distractions, without being "modernized" (for, printing conventions apart, there is no spelling in this text that does not occur at least once in the manuscript). Printed in this way, the poem is not much more difficult to read than Chaucer, and may prove to be accessible to many who have been put off by the typographical oddities of previous editions.

As the title *Sir Gawain and the Green Knight* has no authority except that of the editorial tradition, and as, whatever the *aghlich maister* is, he is hardly a knight, I have substituted the more general word *gome*. This seems to be one of several undifferentiated synonyms for "man", thus leaving his nature open to question. For it *is* a question, and a very important one, in one's attempt to understand the poem; it ought not to be prejudged by the title.

NOTE

A glossary of words that occur frequently in the poem will be found on p. 134. These words are not explained elsewhere, and the reader is advised to learn them.

1 *sesed:* ceased
2 *brittened:* destroyed
  askes: ashes
3 *trammes:* intrigues, plots
5 *Ennias:* Aeneas
  athel: noble
  kinde: kindred
6 *depresed:* subjugated
  patrounes: lords
8 *Fro:* After
  riches him swithe: goes quickly
9 *bobbaunce:* pomp
  bigges: builds
10 *nevenes:* names
  hat: is called
11 *teldes:* dwellings
13 *French flod:* English Channel
15 *winne:* joy
16 *werre:* war
  wrake: distress
17 *By sithes:* At times

18 *blunder:* trouble
19 *Skete:* quickly
  skifted: alternated
  sinne: since then

20 *bigged:* founded
21 *baret:* fighting
22 *turned:* unstable
  tene: harm, trouble
23 *ferlies:* wonders
24 *sin:* since
25 *bult:* dwelt
  Bretain: Britain's
27 *aunter:* adventure
  in erde: on earth
  atle: intend
28 *selly:* wonder
29 *outtrage:* very strange
30 *laye:* poem
31 *astit:* immediately
33 *stad:* established
  stoken: fixed
35 *Loken:* linked, interlocked

SIR GAWAIN

AND THE GRENE GOME

Sithen the sege and the assaut was sesed at Troye,
The burgh brittened and brent to brondes and askes,
The tulk that the trammes of tresoun there wroght
Was tried for his trecherie, the truest on erthe;
5 Hit was Ennias the athel and his highe kinde
That sithen depresed provinces, and patrounes become
Welnegh of al the wele in the west iles.
Fro rich Romulus to Rome riches him swithe,
With gret bobbaunce that burgh he bigges upon first
10 And nevenes hit his owen name, as hit now hat;
Ticius to Tuskan, and teldes begines,
Langaberde in Lumbardie liftes up homes,
And fer over the French flod Felix Brutus
On mony bonkes ful brode Bretain he settes
15   with winne,
        Where werre and wrake and wonder
        By sithes has woned therinne,
        And oft both blisse and blunder
        Ful skete has skifted sinne.

20 And when this Bretain was bigged by this burn rich,
Bolde bredden therinne, baret that loveden,
In mony turned time tene that wroghten.
Mo ferlies on this folde han fallen here oft
Then in any other that I wot, sin that ilk time.
25 Bot of alle that here bult of Bretain kinges
Ay was Arthur the hendest, as I have herde telle.
Forthy an aunter in erde I atle to shewe,
That a selly in sight sum men hit holden,
And an outtrage aventure of Arthures wonderes.
30 If ye wil listen this laye bot one littel while
I shal telle hit astit, as I in toun herde
             with tonge,
        As hit is stad and stoken
        In story stif and stronge,
35   With lel letteres loken,
        In londe so has bene longe.

39 *rekenly:* courteously
40 *rechles:* carefree
42 *Justed:* Jousted
44 *iliche:* alike, the same
45 *avise:* devise
46 *glaum:* noise of revelry
48 *hap:* happiness
50 *samen:* together
51 *kidde:* famous
52 *lovelokkest:* loveliest
 lif haden: lived
53 *comlokest:* most handsome
55 *on sille:* in the hall
56 *hapnest:* most fortunate
57 *of wille:* in temper of mind
58 *gret nye to neven:* very hard
 to name
59 *here:* army
60 *yepe:* fresh
62 *Fro:* After
63 *chauntry:* singing
 cheved: came
64 *clerkes:* priests
65 *Nowel naited onewe:* Christmas celebrated again
 nevened: mentioned
66 *riche:* nobles
 reche hanselle: offer New
 Year gifts
67 *Yeghed:* cried, proclaimed
70 *wroth:* angry, displeased
74 *Guenore:* Guenever
75 *Dressed:* arranged
 dubbed: adorned
76 *Smal:* Fine
 sendal: rich silk
 selure: canopy
77 *tried:* of proven quality
 tolouse: fabric of Toulouse
78 *beten:* set

This king lay at Camilot upon Cristemas
With mony luflich lorde, leudes of the best,
Rekenly of the Rounde Table alle tho rich brether,
40 With rich revel aright and rechles mirthes;
There tournayed tulkes by times ful mony,
Justed ful jolily these gentile knightes,
Sithen cayred to the court, caroles to make.
For there the fest was iliche ful fiften dayes,
45 With alle the mete and the mirthe that men couthe avise;
Such glaum and gle glorious to here,
Dere din upon day, dauncing on nightes,
Al was hap upon high in halles and chambers
With lordes and ladies, as levest him thoght.
50 With alle the wele of the worlde thay woned there samen,
The most kidde knightes under Cristes selven
And the lovelokkest ladies that ever lif haden,
And he the comlokest king that the court holdes;
For al was this fair folk in her first age,
55   on sille,
        The hapnest under heven,
        King highest mon of wille;
        Hit were now gret nye to neven
        So hardy a here on hille.

60 While Newyere was so yepe that hit was new comen,
That day double on the dece was the douth served;
Fro the king was comen with knightes into the halle,
The chauntry of the chapel cheved to an ende;
Loude cry was there cast of clerkes and other,
65 Nowel naited onewe, nevened ful oft;
And sithen riche forth runnen to reche hanselle,
Yeghed yeres-giftes on high, yelde hem by hand,
Debated busily aboute tho giftes;
Ladies laghed ful loude, thogh thay lost haden,
70 And he that wan was not wroth, that may ye wel trowe.
Alle this mirthe thay maden to the mete time.
When thay had washen worthily thay wenten to sete,
The best burn ay above, as hit best semed;
Quene Guenore, ful gay, graithed in the middes,
75 Dressed on the dere dece, dubbed al aboute,
Smal sendal besides, a selure hir over
Of tried tolouse, of tars tapites innowe,
That were enbrawded and beten with the best gemmes

79 *bye:* buy
80 *in day:* ever
81 *comlokest:* fairest lady
   discrye: see
82 *glent:* glanced
83 *A semloker:* one more fair
86 *joifnes:* youth
   childgered: boyish, merry
87 *light:* cheerful
90 *eke:* as well
91 *thurgh nobelay:* in his nobility
   nomen: undertaken
92 *devised:* told
93 *uncouth:* strange
94 *main:* great
95 *alderes:* ancestors
98 *Lede:* Risk
   leve: allow
99 *fulsun:* help
   fairer: advantage
101 *farand:* splendid
103 *fere:* proud
104 *stightles:* stands
    in stalle: in his place
105 *yepe:* young, active
110 *a la dure main:* of the hard hand
113 *Ywan, Uryn son:* Iwain, son of Urien
114 *dight:* set
    derworthly: honourably
116 *crakking:* sudden noise
118 *nakryn:* of kettle-drums
119 *wight:* loud

That might be proved of pris with penies to bye,
        in day;
      The comlokest to discrye
      There glent with ighen gray,
      A semloker that ever he sighe
      Sothe moght no mon say.

85 Bot Arthur wolde not ete til al were served;
   He was so joly of his joifnes, and sumwhat childgered,
   His lif liked him light, he loved the lasse
   Other to long lie or to long sitte,
   So busied him his yong blod and his brain wilde;
90 And also an other maner moved him eke,
   That he thurgh nobelay had nomen, he wolde never ete
   Upon such a dere day, ere him devised were
   Of sum aventurus thing an uncouthe tale,
   Of sum main mervail, that he might trowe,
95 Of alderes, of armes, of other aventures,
   Other sum segg him besoght of sum siker knight
   To joine with him in justing, in jopardy to lay,
   Lede lif for lif, leve uchone other,
   As fortune wolde fulsun hom, the fairer to have.
100 This was the kinges countenaunce where he in court were,
   At uch farand fest among his fre meiny
             in halle.
      Therefore of face so fere
      He stightles stif in stalle,
105   Ful yepe in that Newyere
      Much mirthe he mas with alle.

Thus there stondes in stalle the stif king himselven,
Talkande before the high table of trifles ful hende.
There good Gawain was graithed Guenore beside,
110 And Agravain a la dure main on that other side sittes,
Both the kinges sister-sones, and ful siker knightes.
Bishop Bawdewin above begines the table,
And Ywan, Uryn son, ette with himselven.
These were dight on the dece and derworthly served,
115 And sithen mony siker segg at the sidebordes.
Then the first course come with crakking of trumpes,
With mony baner ful bright that therby henged;
Newe nakryn noise with the noble pipes,
Wilde werbles and wight wakened lote,

120 *hef:* heaved
122 *Foison:* abundance
   freshe: fresh meat
123 *pine:* it was difficult
124 *silveren:* silver dishes
   sere sewes: various stews
127 *lothe:* grudge
129 *ber:* beer
131 *wit:* know
   wont: shortage
133 *liflode:* food
134 *unethe:* hardly
   sesed: ceased
135 *kindely:* properly
136 *hales:* comes
   aghlich: dreadful
137 *on the molde:* on earth
   on mesure: in stature
138 *swire:* neck
   swange: waist
   sware: squarely built
139 *lindes:* loins
140 *etain:* giant
141 *algate:* nevertheless
   minne: say
142 *muckel:* size
143 *al:* although

144 *wombe:* paunch
   wast: waist
   smal: slender
145 *fetures:* parts of his body
   folgande: in proportion
148 *semblaunt:* appearance
   sene: plainly
149 *fade:* bold
150 *overal:* entirely
   enker: bright
152 *strait:* tight
   stek: clung
153 *mensked:* adorned
154 *pelure:* fur
   pured: trimmed
   apert: visible
   pane: lining
155 *blaunner:* fur (ermine?)
157 *Heme:* Neat
   wel-haled: drawn up tight
158 *spenet:* were fastened
   sparlir: calf of leg
159 *bordes:* embroidered strips
   barred: decorated with bars
160 *sholes:* shoes with long
   pointed toes
   under shankes: on his feet

120 That mony hert ful high hef at her towches.
Dainties driven therwith of ful dere metes,
Foison of the freshe, and on so fele dishes
That pine to finde the place the peple beforne
For to sette the silveren that sere sewes halden
125   on clothe;
                Uche leude as he loved himselve
                There laght withouten lothe;
                Ay two had dishes twelve,
                Good ber and bright wine both.

130 Now wil I of hor service say you no more,
For uche wighe may wel wit no wont that there were.
An other noise ful newe neghed bilive,
That the leude might have leve liflode to cach:
For unethe was the noise not a while sesed
135 And the first course in the court kindely served,
There hales in at the halle dore an aghlich maister,
One the most on the molde on mesure high.
Fro the swire to the swange so sware and so thik,
And his lindes and his limmes so long and so gret,
140 Half etain in erde I hope that he were;
Bot mon most I algate minne him to bene,
And that the meriest in his muckel that might ride,
For of bak and of brest al were his body sturn
Both his wombe and his wast were worthily smal,
145 And alle his fetures folgande, in forme that he had,
                ful clene;
                For wonder of his hue men hade,
                Set in his semblaunt sene;
                He ferde as freke were fade,
150   And overal enker grene.

And al graithed in grene this gome and his wedes:
A strait cote ful streght, that stek on his sides,
A mery mantile above, mensked withinne
With pelure pured apert, the pane ful clene,
155 With blithe blaunner ful bright, and his hode both,
That was laght from his lokkes and laide on his shulderes;
Heme wel-haled hose of that same grene
That spenet on his sparlir, and clene spures under
Of bright gold, upon silk bordes barred ful rich,
160 And sholes under shankes there the shalk rides;

17

163 *railed*: arranged
165 *to tor*: too hard
166 *flighes*: insects (butterflies?)
167 *gaudy of grene*: bright green?
168 *payttrure*: breast-trappings
of horse
cropure: crupper, strap pass-
ing round horse's tail
169 *molaines*: ornamented studs
at each end of horse's bit
anamaild: enamelled
171 *arsounes*: saddle-bows
athel: splendid
sturtes: (perhaps copyist's
error for *skurtes*: the
saddle-skirts)
172 *glemered and glent*: gleamed
and glittered
176 *straine*: manage
177 *brawden*: embroidered
178 *gain*: suited
179 *gered*: clothed
180 *here*: hair
of his horse sute: matched
his horse
181 *fannand*: floating
fax: hair
umbefoldes: enfolds

182 *much*: abundant
busk: bush
184 *evesed al umbeturne*: clipped
all round in a circle
185 *halched*: enclosed
186 *capados*: kind of hood
swire: neck
187 *main*: great
188 *cresped*: curled
cemmed: combed
189 *Folden*: Plaited
fildore: gold thread
190 *herle*: strand
here: hair
191 *topping*: forelock
twinnen of a sute: plaited
to match
193 *Dubbed*: adorned
dok: tail
lasted: extended
194 *thrawen*: bound tight
thwong: thong, lace
thwarle: intricate
199 *lait*: lightning
200 *sighe*: saw
202 *drighe*: survive

And alle his vesture veraily was clene verdure.
Both the barres of his belt and other blithe stones
That were richely railed in his aray clene
Aboute himself and his sadel, upon silk werkes,
165 That were to tor for to telle of trifles the half
That were enbrawded above, with briddes and flighes,
With gay gaudy of grene, the gold ay inmiddes.
The pendauntes of his payttrure, the proude cropure,
His molaines, and alle the metail anamaild was then,
170 The stiropes that he stod on stained of the same,
And his arsounes al after and his athel sturtes
That ever glemered and glent al of grene stones;
The fole that he ferkes on fine of that ilke,
             sertain,
175   A grene horse gret and thik,
       A stede ful stif to straine,
       In brawden bridel quik:
       To the gome he was ful gain.

Wel gay was this gome gered in grene,
180 And the here of his hed of his horse sute.
Fair fannand fax umbefoldes his shulderes;
A much berd as a busk over his brest henges,
That with his highlich here that of his hed reches
Was evesed al umbeturne above his elbowes,
185 That half his armes thereunder were halched in the wise
Of a kinges capados that closes his swire.
The mane of that main horse much to hit like,
Wel cresped and cemmed, with knottes ful mony
Folden in with fildore aboute the fair grene,
190 Ay a herle of the here, an other of gold;
The tail and his topping twinnen of a sute,
And bounden both with a bande of a bright grene,
Dubbed with ful dere stones, as the dok lasted,
Sithen thrawen with a thwong a thwarle knot aloft,
195 There mony belles ful bright of brende gold rungen.
Such a fole upon folde, ne freke that him rides,
Was never sene in that sale with sight ere that time
             with ighe.
       He loked as lait so light,
200   So said al that him sighe;
       Hit semed as no mon might
       Under his dintes drighe.

203 *Whether:* Yet
   haubergh: hauberk, coat of mail
204 *pisan:* armour of upper breast and neck
   pented: belonged
206 *holyn bobbe:* cluster, branch of holly
209 *spetos:* cruel
   sparthe: battle-axe
   expoun in spelle: describe in words
210 *elnyerde:* measuring-rod of one ell (45 inches)
211 *grain:* spike
212 *egge:* edge
213 *shapen:* made
   shere: cut
214 *stele:* handle
   hit by gripte: gripped it by
215 *irn:* iron
   wandes: stave's
217 *lapped:* wrapped
   louked: fastened

218 *halme:* handle
   halched: fastened
219 *tried:* fine
   tached: fastened
220 *braiden:* embroidered
221 *heldes him:* comes
222 *dut he no wothe:* he feared no danger
224 *warp:* uttered
225 *ging:* company
229 *reled him:* swaggered
230 *stemmed:* stopped
231 *walt:* possessed
235 *gres:* grass
236 *aumail:* enamel
237 *stalked:* walked cautiously
239 *sellies:* wonders
240 *fairighe:* magic
241 *arghe:* afraid
   athel: noble
242 *stouned:* amazed
   steven: voice
243 *swoghe:* swooning, dead

Whether had he no helme ne haubergh nauther,
Ne no pisan ne no plate that pented to armes,
205 Ne no shafte ne no shelde to showve ne to smite,
Bot in his one hand he had a holyn bobbe,
That is grattest in grene when greves are bare,
And an axe in his other, a huge and unmete,
A spetos sparthe to expoun in spelle whoso might;
210 The hed of an elnyerde the large lenthe had,
The grain al of grene stel and of golde hewen,
The bit burnist bright, with a brode egge
As wel shapen to shere as sharp rasores.
The stele of a stif staf the sturn hit by gripte,
215 That was wounden with irn to the wandes ende,
And al begraven with grene in gracious werkes;
A lace lapped aboute, that louked at the hed,
And so after the halme halched ful oft,
With tried tasseles therto tached innowe
220 On botouns of the bright grene braiden ful rich.
This hathel heldes him in and the halle entres,
Drivande to the high dece, dut he no wothe,
Hailsed he never one, bot high he over loked.
The first word that he warp, "Where is," he said,
225 "The governour of this ging?   Gladly I wolde
Se that segg in sight, and with himself speke
                    resoun."
            To knightes he cast his ighe
            And reled him up and doun;
230   He stemmed, and con studie
            Who walt there most renoun.

There was loking on lenthe the leude to beholde,
For uche mon had mervail what hit mene might,
That a hathel and a horse might such a hue lach,
235 As growe grene as the gres and grener hit semed,
Then grene aumail on golde glowande brighter.
Al studied that there stod, and stalked him nerre
With al the wonder of the worlde what he worch shulde.
For fele sellies had thay sene, bot such never ere;
240 Forthy for fantoum and fairighe the folk there hit demed.
Therfore to answare was arghe mony athel freke,
And al stouned at his steven, and stone-stil seten
In a swoghe silence thurgh the sale rich;

21

244 *slipped upon sleep:* fallen
asleep
slaked: were stilled
245 *in highe:* in haste, suddenly
246 *doute:* fear
248 *loute:* reverence, bow before
249 *cast:* speak
251 *rekenly:* courteously
rad: afraid
253 *hat:* am called
255 *wit:* know
258 *los:* renown
260 *under stel-gere:* in armour
261 *wightest:* most valiant
262 *Preve:* Valiant
laikes: entertainments
263 *kidde:* famous
264 *wained:* brought
266 *pes:* peace
plight: hostility
267 *founded:* journeyed
in fere: in company, with
an army
268 *haubergh:* hauberk, coat of
mail
270 *wene wel:* know well
271 *werre:* fighting
282 *mach:* match
for mightes so waike: because they are so weak
284 *Yol:* Christmas
yepe: vigorous young men

As al were slipped upon slepe, so slaked hor lotes
245   in highe.
       I deme hit not al for doute,
       Bot sum for cortaisie;
       Bot let him that al shulde loute
       Cast unto that wighe.

250 Then Arthur before the high dece that aventure beholdes,
And rekenly him reverenced, for rad was he never,
And said, "Wighe, welcom iwis to this place;
The hed of this hostel Arthur I hat.
Light luflich adoun and lenge, I the praye,
255 And whatso thy wille is we shal wit after."
"Nay, as help me," quoth the hathel, "he that on high sittes,
To wone any while in this wone, hit was not myn erand;
Bot for the los of the, leude, is lift up so high,
And thy burgh and thy burnes best are holden,
260 Stifest under stel-gere on stedes to ride,
The wightest and the worthiest of the worldes kinde,
Preve for to play with in other pure laikes;
And here is kidde cortaisie, as I have herd carp;
And that has wained me hider, iwis, at this time.
265 Ye may be siker by this braunch that I bere here
That I passe as in pes, and no plight seche;
For had I founded in fere in fighting wise,
I have a haubergh at home and a helme both,
A shelde and a sharp spere, shinande bright,
270 And other weppenes to welde, I wene wel, als.
Bot for I wolde no werre, my wedes are softer.
Bot if thou be so bold as alle burnes tellen,
Thou wil grant me goodly the gamen that I ask
           by right."
275   Arthur con answare,
       And said, "Sir cortais knight,
       If thou crave batail bare,
       Here failes thou not to fight."

"Nay, fraist I no fight, in faith I the telle.
280 Hit arn aboute on this bench bot berdles childer;
If I were hasped in armes on a high stede
Here is no mon me to mach, for mightes so waike.
Forthy I crave in this court a Cristemas gamen,
For hit is Yol and New Yere, and here are yepe mony;

286 *brain:* mad
288 *giserne:* battle-axe
290 *bur:* blow
291 *fonde:* attempt
293 *quit-claime:* give up
295 *Elles:* Provided that
    dight me the dome: grant
      me the right
296 *barlay:* I claim it (?)
299 *tite:* quickly
301 *stouned:* amazed
302 *heredmen:* courtiers
303 *rouncy:* horse
    ruched: turned
304 *runishly:* violently
    reled: rolled
305 *bresed:* bristling
    blikkande: shining
306 *Waived:* swept from side to
      side
    waite: look
307 *kepe him with carp:* engage
      him in conversation
308 *rimed him:* cleared his
      throat
    richely: proudly
    right him: prepared himself
310 *rous:* fame
311 *surquidry:* pride
312 *gryndel-laik:* ferocity
    greme: wrath
314 *Overwalt:* overthrown
315 *dares:* cowers
318 *lere:* cheek
319 *wex:* became
    wroth: angry
320 *kene:* bold
    kinde: nature
323 *nise:* foolish
325 *gast:* afraid

285 If any so hardy in this hous holdes himselven,
    Be so bold in his blod, brain in his hed,
    That dar stifly strike a stroke for an other,
    I shal give him of my gift this giserne rich,
    This axe, that is hevy innowe, to handele as him likes,
290 And I shal bide the first bur as bare as I sitte.
    If any freke be so felle to fonde that I telle,
    Lepe lightly me to, and lach this weppen,
    I quit-claime hit for ever, kepe hit as his owen,
    And I shal stonde him a stroke, stif on this flet;
295 Elles thou wil dight me the dome to dele him an other,
                    barlay,
            And yet give him respite
            A twelmonith and a day.
            Now high, and let se tite
300   Dar any herinne oght say."

    If he hem stouned upon first, stiller were then
    Alle the heredmen in halle, the high and the lowe.
    The renk on his rouncy him ruched in his sadel
    And runishly his red ighen he reled aboute,
305 Bende his bresed browes, blikkande grene,
    Waived his berde for to waite whoso wolde rise.
    When none wolde kepe him with carp, he coghed ful high,
    And rimed him ful richely, and right him to speke:
    "What, is this Arthures hous," quoth the hathel then,
310 "That al the rous rennes of thurgh rialmes so mony?
    Where is now your surquidry and your conquestes,
    Your gryndel-laik and your greme, and your gret wordes?
    Now is the revel and the renoun of the Rounde Table
    Overwalt with a word of one wighes speche;
315 For al dares for drede withoute dint shewed."
    With this he laghes so loude that the lord greved;
    The blod shot for shame into his shire face
                    and lere;
            He wex as wroth as winde,
320   So did alle that there were.
            The king as kene by kinde
            Then stod that stif mon nere,

    And said, "Hathel, by heven, thyn asking is nise,
    And as thou foly has fraist, finde the behoves.
325 I know no gome that is gast of thy gret wordes.

25

326 *giserne:* battle-axe
327 *baithen:* grant
    bone: request
330 *halme:* handle
331 *stures:* brandishes
333 *Herre:* taller
335 *drighe:* unmoved
336 *mate:* taken aback
    main: great
340 *con encline:* bowed
341 *sawes sene:* plain words
342 *melly:* contest
343 *worthilich:* honoured
345 *vilany:* discourtesy
    voide: leave
346 *lege:* liege
349 *hevened:* raised
350 *talentif:* eager
352 *hagherer:* more warlike
    of wille: in temperament
353 *baret:* fighting
    rered: raised
354 *wakkest:* weakest
355 *lur:* loss
    who laites: whoever seeks;
      if you want to know
356 *em:* uncle
    to praise: praiseworthy
357 *bounty:* worth
358 *note:* business
    nise: foolish
359 *foldes:* grant
360 *rich:* decide
362 *Riche:* Nobles
    con roun: whispered to-
      gether
363 *redden:* advised
364 *rid:* relieve (of the contest)

Give me now thy giserne, upon Godes halve,
And I shal baithen thy bone that thou boden habbes."
Lightly lepes he him to, and laght at his hand,
Then fersly that other freke upon fote lightis.
330 Now has Arthur his axe, and the halme grippes
And sturnely stures hit aboute, that strike with hit thoght.
The stif mon him before stod upon hight,
Herre then any in the hous by the hed and more.
With sturn chere there he stod he stroked his berde
335 And with a countenaunce drighe he drow doun his cote,
No more mate ne dismaid for his main dintes
Then any burn upon bench had broght him to drink
     of wine.
    Gawain, that sate by the quene,
340
    To the king he con encline,
    "I beseche you now with sawes sene
    This melly mot be mine."

"Wolde ye, worthilich lord," quoth Wawain to the king,
"Bid me bowe fro this bench, and stonde by you there,
345 That I withoute vilany might voide this table,
And that my lege lady liked not ille,
I wolde com to your counsel before your court rich.
For me think hit not semly, as hit is soth knowen,
There such an asking is hevened so high in your sale,
350 Thagh ye yourself be talentif to take hit to yourselven,
While mony so bolde you aboute upon bench sitten,
That under heven, I hope, none hagherer of wille,
Ne better bodies on bent there baret is rered.
I am the wakkest, I wot, and of wit feblest,
355 And lest lur of my lif, who laites the sothe;
Bot for as much as ye are myn em I am only to praise,
No bounty bot your blod I in my body knowe;
And sithen this note is so nise that noght hit you falles,
And I have frained hit at you first, foldes hit to me,
360 And if I carp not comlily, let al this court rich
     bout blame."
    Riche togeder con roun,
    And sithen thay redden alle same:
    To rid the king with croun
365
    And give Gawain the game.

Then comaunded the king the knight for to rise,

367 *ruched him:* prepared himself
372 *Kepe the:* Take care
  kirf: cutting
  sette: apply yourself to
373 *redes:* deal with (attack?)
374 *bur:* blow
375 *giserne:* battle-axe
376 *baist:* was dismayed
  the helder: the more for that
378 *Refourme:* Restate
379 *ethe:* demand
  hattes: art called
380 *trist:* believe
381 *hatte:* am called
385 *on live:* alive; on earth
388 *ferly:* exceedingly
390 *Bigog:* (corruption of) by
  God
391 *fust:* fist
392 *rehersed:* repeated
393 *clanly:* entirely
394 *siker:* assure
396 *foch,* get, take, fetch
398 *wale:* seek
401 *hattes:* art called
402 *ware:* spend, employ
  winne me: find my way
407 *smothely:* courteously

And he ful radly upros, and ruched him fair,
Kneled doun before the king, and caches that weppen;
And he luflily hit him laft, and lifte up his hand,
370 And gave him Godes blessing, and gladly him biddes
That his hert and his hand shulde hardy be both.
"Kepe the, cosin," quoth the king, "that thou on kirf sette,
And if thou redes him right, redily I trowe
That thou shal biden the bur that he shal bede after."
375 Gawain gos to the gome with giserne in hand,
And he boldly him bides, he baist never the helder.
Then carpes to Sir Gawain the knight in the grene,
"Refourme we oure forwardes, ere we firre passe;
First I ethe the, hathel, how that thou hattes,
380 That thou me telle truly, as I trist may."
"In good faith," quoth the good knight, "Gawain I hat,
That bede the this buffet, whatso befalles after,
And at this time twelmonith take at the an other
With what weppen so thou wilt, and with no wigh elles
385   on live."
              That other answares again,
              "Sir Gawain, so mot I thrive,
              As I am ferly fain
              This dint that thou shal drive."

390 "Bigog," quoth the grene knight, "Sir Gawain, me likes
That I shal fang at thy fust that I haf fraist here.
And thou has redily rehersed, by resoun ful true,
Clanly al the covenaunt that I the king asked;
Save that thou shal siker me, segg, by thy trauthe,
395 That thou shal seche me thyself, whereso thou hopes
I may be funde upon folde, and foch the such wages
As thou deles me to-day before this douth rich."
"Where shulde I wale the," quoth Gawain, "where is thy place?
I wot never where thou wones, by him that me wroght,
400 Ne I know not the, knight, thy court ne thy name.
Bot teche me truly thereto, and telle me how thou hattes,
And I shal ware alle my wit to winne me thider,
And that I swere the for sothe, and by my siker trauthe."
"That is innowe in New Yere, hit nedes no more,"
405 Quoth the gome in the grene to Gawain the hende,
"If I the telle truly, when I the tappe have
And thou me smothely has smiten, smartly I the teche
Of my hous and my home and myn owen name,

29

409 *fare:* behaviour
410 *spedes thou the better:* you
will be better off
411 *lait:* seek
412 *slokes:* stop, enough (?)
413 *tole:* weapon
417 *him dresses:* takes his stand
418 *lut with:* bent
lere: flesh
420 *to the note:* to the part
where the short hairs were
422 *kay:* left
424 *shindered:* severed
425 *grece:* flesh
shadde: cut
twinne: two
426 *broun:* shining
428 *foined:* kicked
429 *blikked:* shone
430 *the helder:* the more for that
431 *stithly:* undismayed
432 *runishly:* roughly
raght: reached
435 *stelbawe:* stirrup
436 *here:* hair
437 *sadly:* firmly
438 *unhap:* mishap
ailed: troubled
440 *bluk:* headless trunk
442 *doute:* fear
443 *redde:* declared
445 *dresses:* turns
446 *brode:* with wide-open eyes
448 *hettes:* hast promised
449 *lait:* seek

Then may thou fraist my fare and forwardes holde;
410 And if I spende no speche, then spedes thou the better,
For thou may leng in thy londe and lait no firre,
                    bot slokes.
          Ta now thy grimme tole to the,
          And let se how thou knokes."
415   "Gladly, sir, for sothe,"
          Quoth Gawain; his axe he strokes.

The grene knight upon grounde graithely him dresses,
A littel lut with the hed, the lere he discoveres,
His long lovelich lokkes he laid over his croun,
420 Let the naked nek to the note shewe.
Gawain gripped to his axe, and gederes hit on hight;
The kay fote on the folde he before sette,
Let hit doun lightly light on the naked,
That the sharp of the shalk shindered the bones
425 And shrank thurgh the shire grece, and shadde hit in twinne,
That the bit of the broun stel bot on the grounde.
The fair hed fro the hals hit to the erthe,
That fele hit foined with her fete, there hit forth roled.
The blod braid fro the body, that blikked on the grene;
430 And nauther faltered ne fel the freke never the helder,
Bot stithly he start forth upon stif shankes,
And runishly he raght out, there as renkes stoden,
Laght to his lufly hed, and lift hit up sone,
And sithen bowes to his blonk; the bridel he caches,
435 Steppes into stelbawe and strides aloft,
And his hed by the here in his hand holdes;
And as sadly the segg him in his sadel sette
As non unhap had him ailed, thagh hedles he were
                    in stedde.
440   He braide his bluk aboute,
          That ugly body that bledde;
          Mony one of him had doute,
          By that his resouns were redde.

For the hed in his hand he holdes up even,
445 Toward the derrest on the dece he dresses the face,
And hit lifte up the ighe-liddes and loked ful brode,
And meled thus much with his mouth, as ye may now here:
"Loke, Gawain, thou be graithe to go as thou hettes,
And lait as lelly til thou me, leude, finde,

450 *hette:* promised
451 *thou chose:* that thou goest
   fotte: get
453 *yederly:* promptly
456 *recreaunt:* faint-hearted
457 *runish:* rough, violent
   rout: roar
   raines: reins
458 *Haled:* Went
459 *flagh:* flew
460 *kith:* land, home
   becom: went
461 *fram whethen he was wonnen:*
   from whence he had come
464 *grenne:* grin
465 *breved:* declared
   bare: simply
468 *semblaunt:* indication of his
   feelings
470 *demay:* dismay
472 *laiking of enterludes:* acting
   of plays
473 *kinde:* courtly
474 *dres:* turn
475 *selly:* wonder
   forsake: deny
476 *glent:* glanced
   gainly: courteously
478 *doser:* wall-tapestry
480 *titel therof:* right conferred
   by it.
481 *borde:* table
485 *walt:* spent
   worthed: came
488 *wothe:* danger
   wonde: hesitate

450 As thou has hette in this halle, herande these knightes:
To the grene chapel thou chose, I charge the, to fotte
Such a dint as thou has dalt—deserved thou habbes—
To be yederly yolden on New Yeres morn.
The knight of the grene chapel men knowen me mony;
455 Forthy me for to finde if thou fraistes, failes thou never;
Therfore com, other recreaunt be calde the behoves."
With a runish rout the raines he tornes,
Haled out at the halle dore, his hed in his hand,
That the fire of the flint flagh fro fole hoves.
460 To what kith he becom knew none there,
Never more then thay wiste fram whethen he was wonnen.
What then?
The king and Gawain thare
At that grene thay laghe and grenne;
465 Yet breved was hit ful bare
A mervail among tho menne.

Thagh Arthur the hende king at hert had wonder
He let no semblaunt be sene, bot said ful high
To the comlich quene with cortais speche,
470 "Dere dame, to-day demay you never;
Wel becomes such craft upon Cristemas,
Laiking of enterludes, to laghe and to sing,
Among these kinde caroles of knightes and ladies.
Never the lasse to my mete I may me wel dres,
475 For I have sene a selly, I may not forsake."
He glent upon Sir Gawain, and gainly he said,
"Now sir, heng up thyn axe, that has innowe hewen;"
And hit was done above the dece on doser to henge,
There alle men for mervail might on hit loke
480 And by true titel therof to telle the wonder.
Then thay bowed to a borde these burnes togeder,
The king and the good knight, and kene men hem served
Of alle dainties double, as derrest might falle;
With alle manner of mete and minstralsie both,
485 With wele walt thay that day, til worthed an ende
in londe.
Now thenk wel, Sir Gawain,
For wothe that thou ne wonde
This aventure for to frain
490 That thou has tan on honde.

———

491 *hanselle:* New Year gift
492 *yerned:* longed
    yelping: praise (of valour)
493 *wane:* lacking
494 *stoken of:* abundantly pro-
    vided with
    stafful: cram-full
497 *main:* strong
498 *yirnes:* passes
    yerne: quickly
499 *forme:* beginning
    finisment: end
    foldes: matches, resembles
500 *Yol:* Christmas
    overyede: passed by
501 *serlepes:* in turn
    sued: followed
502 *lentoun:* Lent
504 *weder:* weather
    threpes: contends
505 *clenges adoun:* shrinks down
    (into the earth)
506 *shedes:* falls
507 *flat:* meadowland
510 *solace:* delight
    sues: follows

512 *bolne:* swell
    blowe: bloom
513 *rawes:* hedgerows
    ronk: luxuriant
517 *Zeferus:* Zephyrus, the West
    Wind
    sifles: whistles, blows gently
    sedes: seedlings
    erbes: herbs, green plants
518 *Wela winne:* very joyful
    wort: plant:
    waxes: grows
    theroute: in the open
519 *donkande:* moistening
520 *blush:* gleam
521 *hardenes him:* (the season)
    becomes severe
522 *wax:* grow
524 *flighe:* fly
525 *welkin:* sky
526 *linde:* lime-tree
527 *grayes:* withers
    gres: grass
528 *rotes:* rots
529 *yirnes:* passes

This hanselle has Arthur of aventures on first
In yong yere, for he yerned yelping to here.
Thagh him wordes were wane when thay to sete wenten,
Now are thay stoken of sturn werk, stafful her hand.
495 Gawain was glad to beginne those games in halle,
Bot thagh the ende be hevy, have ye no wonder;
For thagh men ben mery in minde when thay han main drink,
A yere yirnes ful yerne, and yeldes never like,
The forme to the finisment foldes ful selden.
500 Forthy this Yol overyede, and the yere after,
And uche sesoun serlepes sued after other.
After Cristemas com the crabbed lentoun,
That fraistes flesh with the fishe and fode more simple;
Bot then the weder of the worlde with winter hit threpes,
505 Colde clenges adoun, cloudes upliften,
Shire shedes the rain in showres ful warme,
Falles upon fair flat, flowres there shewen,
Both groundes and the greves grene are her wedes,
Briddes busken to bilde, and bremlich singen
510 For solace of the soft somer that sues thereafter
           by bonk;
       And blossumes bolne to blowe
       By rawes rich and ronk,
       Then notes noble innowe
515   Are herde in wod so wlonk.

After, the sesoun of somer with the soft windes,
When Zeferus sifles himself on sedes and erbes;
Wela winne is the wort that waxes theroute,
When the donkande dewe dropes of the leves,
520 To bide a blishful blush of the bright sunne.
Bot then highes hervest, and hardenes him sone,
Warnes him for the winter to wax ful ripe;
He drives with droght the dust for to rise,
Fro the face of the folde to flighe ful high;
525 Wrothe winde of the welkin wrasteles with the sunne,
The leves lancen fro the linde and lighten on the grounde,
And al grayes the gres that grene was ere;
Then al ripes and rotes that ros upon first,
And thus yirnes the yere in yisterdayes mony,

531 *no fage:* no deceit, in truth
532 *Meghelmas mone:* the first new moon after Michaelmas (29th September)
533 *winter wage:* winter's challenge
535 *anious viage:* arduous journey
536 *Al-hal-day:* All Saints' Day (1st November)
537 *fare:* feast
fest: festival, holy day
541 *nevened:* mentioned
542 *japes:* jests
543 *em:* uncle
544 *pertly:* plainly
545 *lege:* liege
546 *cost:* nature
case: affair
kepe: care
547 *tenes:* troubles
never bot trifle: (it is) a mere trifle
548 *boun:* setting out
bur: blow
barely: without delay
to-morn: tomorrow morning

549 *wisse:* guide
551 *Ywan:* Iwain
554 *Boos:* Bohors
Bidver: Bedivere
555 *menskful:* noble (knights)
558 *doel:* grief
559 *Wawain:* Gawain (this form of the name is used to alliterate with *worthy* and *wende*)
560 *drighe:* endure
doelful: painful
563 *wonde:* fear
564 *dere:* grievous
565 *fonde:* try
566 *dowelles:* remains
dresses: prepares
568 *tuly:* made of rich red material, usually silk
tapit: carpet
tight: spread
569 *gere:* armour
glent: glinted
there aloft: on it

530 And winter windes again, as the worlde askes,
                    no fage,
            Til Meghelmas mone
            Was comen with winter wage;
            Then thenkes Gawain ful sone
535   Of his anious viage.

    Yet while Al-hal-day with Arthur he lenges;
    And he made a fare on that fest for the frekes sake,
    With much revel and rich of the Rounde Table.
    Knightes ful cortais and comlich ladies
540 Al for luf of that leude in longing thay were,
    Bot never the lasse ne the later thay nevened bot mirthe;
    Mony joyles for that gentile japes there maden.
    For after mete with mourning he meles to his em,
    And spekes of his passage, and pertly he said,
545 "Now, lege lord of my lif, leve I you ask;
    Ye knowe the cost of this case, kepe I no more
    To telle you tenes thereof, never bot trifle;
    Bot I am boun to the bur barely to-morn
    To seche the gome of the grene, as God wil me wisse."
550 Then the best of the burgh bowed togeder,
            Ywan, and Errik, and other ful mony,
    Sir Doddinaual de Savage, the duk of Clarence,
    Launcelot and Lionel and Lucan the good,
    Sir Boos and Sir Bidver, big men both,
555 And mony other menskful, with Mador de la Port.
    Alle this companie of court com the king nerre
    For to counsel the knight, with care at her hert.
    There was much derf doel driven in the sale
    That so worthy as Wawain shulde wende on that erand,
560 To drighe a doelful dint, and dele no more
                    with bronde.
            The knight made ay good chere
            And said, "What shuld I wonde?
            Of destinies derf and dere
565   What may mon do bot fonde?"

    He dowelles there al that day, and dresses on the morn,
    Askes erly his armes, and alle thay were broght.
    First a tuly tapit tight over the flet,
    And rich was the gilt gere that glent there aloft;
570 The stif mon steppes theron and the stel handeles,

37

571 *Dubbed:* arrayed
tars: silk of Tharsia
572 *crafty:* skilfully made
capados: kind of hood
573 *blaunner:* fur (ermine?)
574 *sabatouns:* steel shoes
575 *lapped:* wrapped
greves: armour for shins
576 *polaines:* armour for knees
piched: attached
577 *knaged:* fastened
578 *Queme:* comfortable
quissewes: armour for thighs
579 *thrawen:* sinewy
thwonges: thongs, laces
tached: fastened
580 *brawden:* linked
bruny: shirt of mail
581 *Umbeweved:* enveloped
582 *brace:* armour for arms
583 *cowters:* elbow-pieces
584 *goodlich:* goodly
gere: armour
gain: be of use to
586 *cote-armure:* coat, richly embroidered, worn over the armour
587 *spend:* fastened
589 *sain:* girdle
umbe: about
590 *harnais:* armour
593 *auter:* altar
594 *feres:* companions

596 *conveyed:* escorted
bekende: commended
598 *frenges:* fringes
599 *nailet:* studded with nails
note: purpose
riched: prepared
600 *barred:* decorated with bars
601 *apparail:* adornment
paittrure: breast-trappings of horse
602 *cropure:* crupper
covertour: horse-cloth
accorded with: matched
arsounes: saddle-bows
603 *railed:* arranged
on red: on a red background
604 *glent:* glinted
glem: radiance
608 *lightly:* light
urison: embroidered covering on helmet.
aventail: movable front of helmet
610 *borde:* embroidered strip
semes: ornamental stitching about the seams
611 *papiaies:* parrots
perning: preening
betwene: at intervals
612 *Tortors:* turtledoves
truelofes: true-love knots
entailed: depicted

Dubbed in a dublet of a dere tars,
And sithen a crafty capados, closed aloft,
That with a bright blaunner was bounden withinne.
Then set thay the sabatouns upon the segge fotes,
575 His legges lapped in stel with luflich greves,
With polaines piched thereto, polised ful clene,
Aboute his knes knaged with knotes of gold;
Queme quissewes then, that quaintlich closed
His thik thrawen thighes, with thwonges to tached;
580 And sithen the brawden bruny of bright stel ringes
Umbeweved that wigh upon wlonk stuffe,
And wel burnist brace upon his both armes,
With good cowters and gay, and gloves of plate,
And alle the goodlich gere that him gain shulde
585   that tide;
          With rich cote-armure,
          His gold spures spend with pride,
          Girde with a bronde ful sure
          With silk sain umbe his side.

590 When he was hasped in armes, his harnais was rich;
The lest lachet other loupe lemed of golde.
So harnaist as he was he herknes his masse,
Offred and honoured at the high auter.
Sithen he comes to the king and to his court-feres,
595 Laches lufly his leve at lordes and ladies;
And thay him kist and conveyed, bekende him to Crist.
By that was Gringolet graith, and girde with a sadel
That glemed ful gaily with mony gold frenges,
Aywhere nailet ful newe, for that note riched;
600 The bridel barred aboute, with bright gold bounden;
The apparail of the paittrure and of the proude skirtes,
The cropure and the covertour, accorded with the arsounes;
And al was railed on red rich gold nailes,
That al glitered and glent as glem of the sunne.
605 Then hentes he the helme, and hastily hit kisses,
That was stapled stifly, and stoffed withinne;
Hit was high on his hed, hasped behinde,
With a lightly urisoun over the aventaile,
Enbrawden and bounden with the best gemmes
610 On brode silkin borde, and briddes on semes,
As papiaies painted perning betwene,
Tortors and truelofes entailed so thik

39

615 *cercle:* circlet
616 *unbeclipped:* surrounded
618 *broun:* gleaming
619 *goules:* gules, red
620 *depaint:* painted
622 *semlily:* becomingly
623 *apendes:* belongs
625 *Salamon:* Solomon
   sumwhile: once
626 *In betokning:* as a symbol
628 *umbelappes:* enfolds
   loukes: locks
630 *Overal:* everywhere
631 *accordes to:* befits
632 *five and sere five:* five times
   five
   sithes: ways
634 *Voided of:* free from
   ennurned: adorned
   in mote: in the castle
642 *afiaunce:* trust
644 *melly:* battle
   was stad: stood
645 *thro:* intense
   thurgh alle other thinges:
   above all else
648 *At this cause:* for this reason
   comliche: fittingly
649 *depainted:* painted
650 *blushed:* glanced
   belde: courage
   paired: failed
652 *fraunchise:* generosity
   felaghship: love of his fel-
   lowmen
   forbe: more than
653 *clannes:* purity

As mony burde theraboute had bene seven winter
                         in toune.
615   The cercle was more o pris
               That umbeclipped his croun,
               Of diamauntes a devis
               That both were bright and broun.

      Then thay shewed him the shelde, that was of shire goules
620   With the pentangel depaint of pure gold hues.
      He braides hit by the bauderik, aboute the hals castes,
      That besemed the segg semlily fair.
      And why the pentangel apendes to that prince noble
      I am intent you to telle, thogh tary hit me shulde:
625   Hit is a signe that Salamon set sumwhile
      In betokning of trauthe, by title that hit habbes,
      For hit is a figure that haldes five pointes,
      And uche line umbelappes and loukes in other,
      And aywhere hit is endeles; and Englich hit callen
630   Overal, as I here, the endeles knot.
      Forthy hit accordes to this knight and to his clere armes,
      For ay faithful in five and sere five sithes
      Gawain was for good knowen, and as gold pured,
      Voided of uche vilany, with vertues ennurned
635   in mote;
               Forthy the pentangel newe
               He ber in shelde and cote,
               As tulk of tale most true
               And gentilest knight of lote.

640   First he was founden fautles in his five wittes,
      And eft failed never the freke in his five fingeres,
      And alle his afiaunce upon folde was in the five woundes
      That Crist caght on the cros, as the crede telles;
      And wheresoever this mon in melly was stad,
645   His thro thoght was in that, thurgh alle other thinges,
      That alle his fersnes he feng at the five joyes
      That the hende heven quene had of hir childe;
      At this cause the knight comliche had
      In the more half of his shelde hir image depainted,
650   That when he blushed thereto his belde never paired.
      The fift five that I finde that the freke used
      Was fraunchise and felaghship forbe al thing,
      His clannes and his cortaisie croked were never,

654 *pointes:* qualities
655 *happed:* fastened
656 *sithes:* kinds (of virtue)
   fetled: arranged
657 *halched in:* joined to
658 *fiched:* fixed
659 *samned:* came together
660 *noke:* corner
661 *glod:* came
662 *shene:* bright
   shapen: made
663 *goules:* gules, red
669 *wende:* thought
670 *sperred:* struck
671 *stroke:* was struck
672 *semly:* comely knight
   siked: sighed
673 *al same:* together
   til: to
674 *scathe:* a great pity
676 *fere:* equal
677 *Warloker:* more carefully
678 *dight:* appointed
   worthed: been made
679 *lowande:* brilliant
   semes: would suit
680 *brittened:* destroyed
681 *Hadet:* beheaded
   alvish: elvish
   angardes: of vanity
683 *cavelaciouns:* triflings
684 *waltered:* flowed plentifully
685 *semly:* comely
687 *abode:* stay, delay
688 *wightly:* swiftly
689 *wilsum:* bewildering, mis-
   leading
691 *Logres:* England
693 *leudles:* companionless
694 *fare:* food

And pity, that passes alle pointes, these pure five
655 Were harder happed on that hathel then on any other.
Now alle these five sithes, for sothe, were fetled on this knight,
And uchone halched in other, that none ende had,
And fiched upon five pointes, that failed never,
Ne samned never in no side, ne sundred nauther,
660 Withouten ende at any noke aywhere founde,
Where-ever the gamen began, or glod to an ende.
Therfore on his shene shelde shapen was the knot
Royally with red gold upon red goules,
That is the pure pentangel with the peple called
665   with lore.
    Now graithed is Gawain gay,
    And laght his lance right thore,
    And gef hem alle good day,
    He wende for ever more.

670 He sperred the stede with the spures and sprong on his way,
So stif that the stone-fire stroke out thereafter.
Al that segh that semly siked in hert,
And said sothely al same segges til other,
Carande for that comly: "By Crist, hit is scathe
675 That thou, leude, shal be lost, that art of lif noble;
To finde his fere upon folde, in faith, is not ethe.
Warloker to have wroght had more wit bene,
And have dight yonder dere a duk to have worthed;
A lowande leder of leudes in londe him wel semes,
680 And so had better have bene than brittened to noght,
Hadet with an alvish mon, for angardes pride.
Who knew ever any king such counsel to take
As knightes in cavelaciouns on Cristemas games!"
Wel much was the warme water that waltered of ighen,
685 When that semly sire soght fro tho wones
    that day.
    He made none abode,
    Bot wightly went his way;
    Mony wilsum way he rode,
690   The boke as I herde say.

Now rides this renk thurgh the rialme of Logres,
Sir Gawain, on Godes halve, thagh him no gamen thoght.
Oft leudles alone he lenges on nightes
There he founde noght him before the fare that he liked.

43

695 *fere:* companion
frithes: woods
downes: hills
698 *lift:* left
699 *forlondes:* promontories
701 *Wirale:* Wirral
lite: few
706 *nikked him with nay:* answered "No" to him
710 *unbene:* dreary
713 *overclambe:* climbed over
contrayes: regions
714 *floten:* having wandered
fremedly: as a stranger
715 *warthe:* river-side
716 *foo:* foe
bot ferly hit were: or else it was a wonder (i.e. there were few exceptions)
718 *by mount:* among the hills
719 *to tor:* too hard
dole: part, fraction
720 *sumwhile:* sometimes
wormes: dragons
werres: battles

721 *wodwos:* wild men of the woods
knarres: gnarled rocks
722 *beres:* bears
bores: boars
723 *etaines:* giants
anelede: pursued
felle: steep rock
724 *Nade he:* had he not
drighe: patient
725 *dreped:* beaten up
726 *werre:* fighting
wrathed: upset
727 *shadde:* fell
728 *fres:* froze
fale: faded
729 *slete:* sleet
irnes: armour
731 *crest:* mountain-top
borne: stream
732 *iisse-ikkles:* icicles
733 *plites:* conditions
734 *By contray:* across country

695 Had he no fere bot his fole by frithes and downes,
    Ne no gome bot God by gate with to carp,
    Til that he neghed ful negh into the Northe Wales.
    Alle the iles of Anglesay on lift half he haldes,
    And fares over the fordes by the forlondes,
700 Over at the Holy Hed, til he had eft bonk
    In the wildrenesse of Wirale; woned there bot lite
    That other God other gome with good hert loved.
    And ay he frained, as he ferde, at frekes that he met,
    If thay had herde any carp of a knight grene,
705 In any grounde theraboute, of the grene chapel;
    And al nikked him with nay, that never in her live
    Thay seghe never no segg that was of such hues
            of grene.
        The knight tok gates straunge
710   In mony a bonk unbene,
        His chere ful oft con chaunge
        That chapel ere he might sene.

Mony cliff he overclambe in contrayes straunge,
    Fer floten fro his frendes fremedly he rides;
715 At uche warthe other water there the wighe passed
    He founde a foo him before, bot ferly hit were,
    And that so foule and so felle that fight him behoved.
    So mony mervail by mount there the mon findes
    Hit were to tor for to telle of the tenthe dole.
720 Sumwhile with wormes he werres, and with wolves als,
    Sumwhile with wodwos, that woned in the knarres,
    Both with bulles and beres, and bores otherwhile,
    And etaines, that him anelede of the high felle;
    Nade he bene dughty and drighe, and Drightin had served,
725 Douteles he had bene ded and dreped ful oft.
    For werre wrathed him not so much, that winter was wors,
    When the colde clere water fro the cloudes shadde,
    And fres ere hit falle might to the fale erthe;
    Nere slain with the slete he sleped in his irnes
730 Mo nightes then innowe in naked rokkes,
    There as claterande fro the crest the colde borne rennes,
    And henged high over his hed in hard iisse-ikkles.
    Thus in peril and paine and plites ful hard
    By contray cayres this knight, til Cristemas even,
735   alone;

45

738 *rede:* direct, advise
739 *wisse:* direct
741 *ferly:* amazingly
742 *holtwodes:* woods
743 *hore:* hoar, grey
744 *haghthorne:* hawthorn
   harled al samen: tangled
      together
745 *raged:* shaggy
   railed: arrayed
747 *pine:* pain
748 *glides:* hastens
749 *misy:* bog
   mire: swamp
750 *costes:* conduct
   kever: manage
752 *baret:* strife, trouble
   quelle: terminate
753 *siking:* sighing
755 *herber:* lodging
   heghly: devoutly
756 *to-morn:* tomorrow morning
757 *thereto:* for this purpose.
   prestly: promptly
761 *sained him:* crossed himself
   in sithes sere: several times
762 *spede:* prosper, help

763 *Nade he:* he had not
   thrie: thrice
764 *was ware of:* perceived
   mote: moat
765 *lawe:* mound
   loken: shut in
   boghs: boughs
766 *borelich:* massive
   bole: tree-trunk
767 *comlokest:* most comely
   aght: owned
768 *Piched:* erected
   praiere: meadow
769 *piked palais:* palisade with
      spikes
   pined: enclosed
770 *umbeteghe:* surrounded
771 *holde:* stronghold, castle
   avised: contemplated
772 *shemered:* shimmered
774 *Sain Gilian:* St Julian
      (l'Hospitalier)
775 *cortaisly had him kidde:* had
      treated him courteously
776 *bone hostel:* a good lodging
   yette: grant

                    The knight wel that tide
                    To Mary made his mone,
                    That ho him rede to ride
                    And wisse him to sum wone.

740 By a mount on the morn merily he rides
    Into a forest ful depe, that ferly was wilde,
    High hilles on uche a half, and holtwodes under
    Of hore okes ful huge a hundreth togeder;
    The hasel and the haghthorne were harled al samen,
745 With rugh raged mosse railed aywhere,
    With mony briddes unblithe upon bare twiges,
    That pitously there piped for pine of the colde.
    The gome upon Gringolet glides hem under,
    Thurgh mony misy and mire, mon al him one,
750 Carande for his costes, lest he ne kever shulde
    To se the service of that sire, that on that self night
    Of a burde was borne oure baret to quelle;
    And therefore siking he said, "I beseche the, lord,
    And Mary, that is mildest moder so dere,
755 Of sum herber there highly I might here masse,
    And thy matines to-morn, mekely I ask,
    And therto prestly I pray my Pater and Ave
                    and crede."
                    He rode in his prayere,
760   And cried for his misdede;
                    He sained him in sithes sere
                    And said, "Cros Crist me spede."

    Nade he sained himself, segg, bot thrie,
    Ere he was ware in the wod of a wone in a mote,
765 Above a launde, on a lawe, loken under boghs
    Of mony borelich bole aboute by the diches:
    A castel the comlokest that ever knight aght,
    Piched on a praiere, a park al aboute,
    With a piked palais pined ful thik,
770 That umbeteghe mony tre mo then two mile.
    That holde on that one side the hathel avised,
    As hit shemered and shon thurgh the shire okes;
    Then has he hendely of his helme, and highly he thonkes
    Jesus and Sain Gilian, that gentile are both,
775 That cortaisly had him kidde, and his cry herkened.
    "Now bone hostel," quoth the burn, "I beseche you yette!"

777 *gerdes:* strikes his spurs
778 *chauncely:* by chance
chosen: gone
781 *upbraide:* pulled up
782 *stoken:* shut
783 *arayed:* constructed
784 *dut:* feared
785 *hoved:* stopped
787 *wod:* stood (waded)
788 *haled:* rose
on loft: aloft
789 *tables:* projecting cornice-moulding
790 *Enbaned:* fortified
in the best lawe: in accordance with the best rules
791 *garites:* watch-towers
gered: constructed
betwene: at intervals
792 *loupe:* window
louked: fastened
793 *barbican:* outer fortification
blushed: looked
794 *innermore:* further in
795 *telded:* set up
betwene: at intervals
trochet: battlemented
796 *filioles:* pinnacles
fighed: fitted
ferlily: wonderfully

797 *corven:* carved
coprounes: ornamental tops
sleghe: skilfully made
798 *ches:* noticed
799 *bastel roves:* roofs of towers
blenked: gleamed
800 *poudred:* scattered
801 *carneles:* openings in the battlements
clambred: clustered
802 *papure:* paper
804 *kever:* manage
cloister: enclosure
805 *herber:* lodge
806 *avinant:* pleasant
809 *nome:* took
810 *erraunt:* travelling (on a mission)
811 *myn erand:* as my messenger
812 *herber:* lodging
813 *Peter:* by St Peter
815 *yare:* nimbly
swithe: quickly
816 *frely:* courteously
817 *draught:* drawbridge
derely: courteously

Then gerdes he to Gringolet with the gilt heles,
And he ful chauncely has chosen to the chef gate,
That broght bremely the burn to the brige ende
780   in haste.
        The brige was breme upbraide,
        The gates were stoken faste,
        The walles were wel arayed,
        Hit dut no windes blaste.

785 The burn bode on bonk, that on blonk hoved,
Of the depe double dich that drof to the place;
The walle wod in the water wonderly depe,
And eft a ful huge hight hit haled up on loft,
Of hard hewen stone up to the tables,
790 Enbaned under the abatailment in the best lawe;
And sithen garites ful gay gered betwene,
With mony luflich loupe that louked ful clene;
A better barbican that burn blushed upon never.
And innermore he behelde that halle ful high,
795 Towres telded betwene, trochet ful thik,
Fair filioles that fighed, and ferlily long,
With corven coprounes craftily sleghe.
Chalkwhite chimnies there ches he innowe
Upon bastel roves, that blenked ful white.
800 So mony pinakle paintet was poudred aywhere,
Among the castel carneles clambred so thik,
That pared out of papure purely hit semed.
The fre freke on the fole hit fair innowe thogh·
If he might kever to com the cloister withinne
805 To herber in that hostel while haliday lested,
               avinant.
        He calde, and sone there com
        A porter pure plesaunt,
        On the walle his erand he nome,
810   And hailsed the knight erraunt.

"Good sir," quoth Gawain, "woldes thou go myn erand
To the high lord of this hous, herber to crave?"
"Ye, Peter," quoth the porter, "and purely I trowe
That ye be, wighe, welcom to wone while you likes."
815 Then yede that wighe yare, and com again swithe,
And folk frely him with, to fange the knight.
Thay let doun the gret draght and derely out yeden,

820 *yolden him:* allowed him to pass
yarked: raised
821 *rekenly:* courteously
822 *Sere:* several
824 *swieres:* esquires
826 *hef:* lifted
828 *blasoun:* shield
831 *wonnen:* brought
833 *loutes:* comes
834 *mensk:* courtesy
836 *to have at your will and welde:* to use as you please
839 *foryelde:* reward
841 *felde:* fold, embrace
842 *glight:* looked
gret: greeted
843 *aght:* owned
844 *for the nones:* indeed
of high elde: of advanced age
845 *bever-hued:* reddish brown

846 *stif on the strithe:* standing firmly
shankes: legs
848 *semed:* suited
849 *in lee:* in peace and security
850 *him charred:* turned
852 *boun:* ready
bode: command
853 *boure:* bedroom
855 *covertoures:* coverlets
curious: elaborately patterned
panes: panels of materials of different colours
856 *blaunner:* fur (ermine?)
857 *Rudeles:* curtains
858 *Tapites:* tapestries
tight to: hung on
wowe: wall
tuly: rich red material
tars: silk of Tharsia
859 *of folgande sute:* of similar sort

And kneled doun on her knes upon the colde erthe
To welcom this ilk wighe as worthy hom thoght;
820 Thay yolden him the brode gate, yarked up wide,
And he hem raised rekenly, and rode over the brige.
Sere segges him sesed by sadel, while he light,
And sithen stabeled his stede stif men innowe.
Knightes and swieres comen doun then
825 For to bring this burn with blisse into halle;
When he hef up his helme there highed innowe
For to hent hit at his hand, the hende to serven;
His bronde and his blasoun both thay token.
Then hailsed he ful hendely tho hatheles uchone,
830 And mony proud mon there presed that prince to honour.
Alle hasped in his high wede to halle thay him wonnen,
There fair fire upon flet fersly brenned.
Then the lord of the leude loutes fro his chamber
For to mete with mensk the mon on the flor;
835 He said, "Ye are welcom to welde as you likes;
That here is, al is you owen, to have at your wille
                    and welde."
             "Grant merci," quoth Gawain,
             "There Crist hit you foryelde."
840   As frekes that semed fain
             Aither other in armes con felde.

Gawain glight on the gome that goodly him gret,
And thoght hit a bold burn that the burgh aght,
A huge hathel for the nones, and of high elde;
845 Brode, bright was his berde, and al bever-hued,
Sturn, stif on the strithe on stalworth shankes,
Felle face as the fire, and fre of his speche;
And wel him semed, for sothe, as the segg thoght,
To lede a lordship in lee of leudes ful good.
850 The lord him charred to a chamber, and chefly comaundes
To deliver him a leude, him lowly to serve;
And there were boun at his bode burnes innowe
That broght him to a bright boure, there bedding was noble,
Of cortaines of clene silk with clere gold hemmes,
855 And covertoures ful curious with comlich panes,
Of bright blaunner above enbrawded besides,
Rudeles rennande on ropes, red gold ringes,
Tapites tight to the wowe of tuly and tars,
And under fete, on the flet, of folgande sute.

861 *bruny:* shirt of mail
862 *rad:* promptly
863 *charge:* take possession of
864 *happed:* wrapped
865 *sailande:* flowing
866 *ver:* springtime
    visage: appearance
868 *Lowande:* brilliant
869 *comloker:* more comely
871 *Whethen:* from wherever
873 *pere:* equal
875 *cheier:* chair
877 *Quissines:* cushions
    queldepointes: quilted covers
879 *bleaunt:* a rich material
881 *ennurned:* adorned
882 *settel:* seat
    semlich: becomingly
883 *achaufed:* warmed
    chefly: quickly
    mende: improved
884 *telded up:* set up
    trestes: trestles
886 *Sanap:* protective cloth over
    tablecloth
    salure: salt-cellar
889 *sere:* various
    sewes: stews
    sete: appropriate
890 *Double-felde:* in double
    helpings
    fele kin: many kinds of
891 *brad:* grilled
    gledes: red-hot coals
892 *sothen:* boiled
    sewe: stew
893 *sawes:* sauce
    sleghe: skilfully made
895 *rehaited:* urged

860 There he was dispoiled, with speches of mirthe,
The burn of his bruny, and of his bright wedes.
Rich robes ful rad renkes him broghten,
For to charge and to chaunge and chose of the best.
Sone as he one hent, and happed therinne,
865 That sete on him semly with sailande skirtes,
The ver by his visage verayly hit semed
Welnegh to uche hathel, alle on hues,
Lowande and lufly alle his limmes under,
That a comloker knight never Crist made,
870   hem thoght.
             Whethen in worlde he were,
             Hit semed as he moght
             Be prince withouten pere
             In felde there felle men foght.

875 A cheier before the chimny, there charcole brenned,
Was graithed for Sir Gawain graithely with clothes,
Quissines upon queldepointes that quaint were both;
And then a mery mantile was on that mon cast
Of a broun bleaunt, enbrawded ful rich
880 And fair furred withinne with felles of the best,
Alle of ermin ennurned, his hode of the same;
And he sete in that settel semlich rich,
And achaufed him chefly, and then his chere mended.
Sone was telded up a table on trestes ful fair,
885 Clad with a clene clothe that clere white shewed,
Sanap, and salure, and silverin spones.
The wighe weshe at his wille, and went to his mete.
Segges him served semly innowe
With sere sewes and sete, sesounde of the best,
890 Double-felde, as hit falles, and fele kin fishes:
Sum baken in bred, sum brad on the gledes,
Sum sothen, sum in sewe savoured with spices,
And ay sawes so sleghe that the segg liked.
The freke calde hit a fest ful frely and oft
895 Ful hendely, when alle the hatheles rehaited him at ones
                     as hende:
             "This penaunce now ye take,
             And eft hit shal amende."
             That mon much mirthe con make,
900   For wine in his hed that wende.

901 *spied:* inquired
   spured: asked
   upon spare wise: tactfully
902 *privy pointes:* discreet questions
903 *beknew:* acknowledged
904 *athel:* noble
907 *case:* chance
   limped: befell
910 *mote:* castle
911 *prestly:* promptly
912 *thewes:* manners
913 *Apendes:* belongs
914 *molde:* earth
   mensk: fame
915 *fere:* companion
916 *semlich:* pleasantly
   sleghtes: skilful deeds
   thewes: knightly conduct
917 *techeles:* spotless
918 *speed:* profit
   unspured: without asking
919 *sin:* since
   nurture: good breeding
922 *burthe:* birth
924 *mere:* noble
932 *hersum:* devout
933 *loutes:* turns
934 *closet:* closed pew
935 *glides:* hastens
936 *lappe:* loose end or fold of dress, lapel
937 *couthly:* with familiarity
939 *throly:* heartily
   halched: embraced
940 *samen:* together
942 *closet:* closed pew

Then was spied and spured upon spare wise
By privy pointes of that prince, put to himselven,
That he beknew cortaisly of the court that he were,
That athel Arthur the hende holdes him one,
905 That is the rich royal king of the Rounde Table,
And hit was Wawain himself that in that wone sittes,
Comen to that Cristemas, as case him then limped.
When the lord had lerned that he the leude had,
Loude laghed he therat, so lef hit him thoght,
910 And alle the men in that mote maden much joy
To apere in his presense prestly that time,
That alle pris and prowes and pured thewes
Apendes to his persoun, and praised is ever,
Before alle men upon molde his mensk is the most.
915 Uche segg ful softly said to his fere:
"Now shal we semlich se sleghtes of thewes
And the techeles termes of talking noble;
Wich speed is in speche unspured may we lerne,
Sin we have fanged that fine fader of nurture.
920 God has geven us his grace goodly for sothe,
That such a gest as Gawain grantes us to have,
When burnes blithe of his burthe shal sitte
                    and singe.
          In mening of maneres mere
925   This burn now shal us bring;
          I hope that may him here
          Shal lerne of luf-talking."

By that the diner was done and the dere up
Hit was negh at the night neghed the time.
930 Chaplaines to the chapeles chosen the gate,
Rungen ful richely, right as thay shulden,
To the hersum evensong of the high tide.
The lord loutes therto, and the lady als,
Into a comly closet quaintly ho entres.
935 Gawain glides ful gay and gos theder sone;
The lord laches him by the lappe and ledes him to sitte,
And couthly him knowes and calles him his name,
And said he was the welcomest wighe of the worlde.
And he him thonked throly, and aither halched other,
940 And seten soberly samen the service while.
Then list the lady to loke on the knight,
Then com ho of hir closet with mony clere burdes;

943 *lyre:* face
944 *compas:* proportion
costes: nature
945 *wener:* more lovely
Wenore: Guenever
946 *ches:* went
chaunsel: chancel
cherish: salute graciously
947 *lift:* left
951 *yepe:* fresh, young
yolwe: yellow, withered
952 *railed:* arranged
953 *ronkled:* wrinkled
rolled: hung in loose folds
956 *shedes:* falls
957 *gorger:* neckerchief
gered: clothed
swire: neck
958 *chimbled:* wrapped up
959 *frount:* forehead
enfoubled: muffled up
960 *Toret:* turreted
treieted: adorned
962 *nase:* nose
963 *sellily:* exceedingly
964 *mensk:* worthy
molde: earth

967 *balgh:* bulging? (but the word does not usually have this meaning: perhaps MS form *bay*, previously thought to be erroneous, is correct in the sense "protruding"— like a bay-window)
968 *likkerwis:* delightful
on to lik: to take pleasure in
969 *on lode:* with her, in tow
970 *glight:* looked
971 *againes:* towards
972 *heldande:* bowing
973 *lovelokker:* more lovely
lappes: embraces
975 *callen him of:* beg for
979 *unsparely:* plentifully
980 *winnelich:* pleasant
982 *Minned:* urged
sithes: occasions
983 *highly:* gaily
984 *waived hom:* urged them with gestures
worship therof: honour of gaining possession of it

Ho was fairest in felle, of flesh and of lyre,
And of compas and colour and costes, of alle other,
945 And wener then Wenore, as the wighe thoght.
He ches thurgh the chaunsel to cherish that hende.
An other lady hir ladde by the lift hand,
That was alder then ho, an auncian hit semed,
And highly honoured with hatheles aboute.
950 Bot unlike on to loke tho ladies were,
For if the yonge was yepe, yolwe was that other;
Rich red on that one railed aywhere,
Rugh ronkled chekes that other on rolled;
Kerchofes of that one, with mony clere perles,
955 Hir brest and hir bright throte bare displayed,
Shon shirer then snaw that shedes on hilles;
That other with a gorger was gered over the swire,
Chimbled over hir blak chin with chalkwhite vailes,
Hir frount folden in silk, enfoubled aywhere,
960 Toret and treieted with trifles aboute,
That noght was bare of that burde bot the blak browes,
The twaine ighen and the nase, the naked lippes,
And those were soure to se and sellily blered.
A mensk lady on molde mon may hir calle,
965   for God!
          Hir body was short and thik,
          Hir buttokes balgh and brode;
          More likkerwis on to lik
          Was that sho had on lode.

970 When Gawain glight on that gay, that graciously loked,
With leve laght of the lord he went hem againes;
The alder he hailses, heldande ful lowe,
The loveloker he lappes a littel in armes,
He kisses hir comlily, and knightly he meles.
975 Thay callen him of aquointaunce, and he hit quik askes
To be her servaunt sothly, if hemself liked.
Thay tan him betwene hem, with talking him leden
To chamber, to chimny, and chefly thay asken
Spices, that unsparely men speded hom to bring,
980 And the winnelich wine therwith uche time.
The lord luflich aloft lepes ful oft,
Minned mirthe to be made upon mony sithes,
Hent highly of his hode, and on a spere henged,
And waived hom to winne the worship therof,

57

986 *fonde:* try
filter: contend, struggle in the crowd
987 *me wont:* I have to lose
988 *tait:* merry
993 *nime:* take
994 *him dight:* went
995 *minnes:* thinks of
996 *dighe:* die
997 *waxes:* increases
998 *dainties:* delights
999 *messe:* snack
mele: mealtime
1000 *drest:* arranged
1002 *lent:* took his place
1004 *Even:* in places of equal honour
messe: food
metely: duly
1005 *semed:* was fitting
1006 *grome:* man
1007 *tene:* trouble
1008 *pointe:* describe in detail
pined me: troubled myself
paraventure: perhaps
1010 *wale:* choice, excellent
1012 *derne:* private
1014 *was passande:* surpassed
1015 *in vaires:* in truth
1016 *Trumpes:* trumpets
nakeris: kettle-drums
1017 *repaires:* is present
1018 *tented:* attended to
1020 *dut:* joy
1021 *as thro:* with all boldness
thronge in: pressed on
1022 *Sain Jones Day:* St John's Day (27 December)
1023 *laik:* entertainment

985   That most mirthe might meve that Cristemas while;
"And I shal fonde, by my faith, to filter with the best,
Ere me wont the wede with help of my frendes."
Thus with laghande lotes the lord hit tait makes,
For to glade Sir Gawain with games in halle
990   that night,
        Til that hit was time
        The lord comaunded light;
        Sir Gawain his leve con nime
        And to his bed him dight.

995   On the morn, as uche mon minnes that time
That Drightin for oure destiny to dighe was borne,
Wele waxes in uche a wone in worlde for his sake;
So did hit there on that day thurgh dainties mony.
Both at messe and at mele messes full quaint
1000 Derf men upon dece drest of the best.
The olde auncian wif highest ho sittes,
The lord lufly her by lent, as I trowe;
Gawain and the gay burde togeder thay seten,
Even inmiddes, as the messe metely come,
1005 And sithen thurgh al the sale, as hem best semed,
By uche grome at his degree graithely was served.
There was mete, there was mirthe, there was much joy,
That for to telle thereof hit me tene were,
And to pointe hit yet I pined me paraventure.
1010 Bot yet I wot that Wawain and the wale burde
Such comfort of her companie caghten togeder
Thurgh the dere daliaunce of her derne wordes,
With clene cortais carp closed fro filthe,
That hor play was passande uche prince gamen,
1015   in vaires.
        Trumpes and nakeris,
        Much piping there repaires;
        Uche mon tented his
        And thay two tented thaires.

1020 Much dut was there driven that day and that other,
And the thrid as thro thronge in therafter;
The joy of Sain Jones day was gentile to here,
And was the last of the laik, leudes there thoghten.
There were gestes to go upon the gray morn,
1025 Forthy wonderly thay woke, and the wine dronken,

1026 *drighly:* unceasingly
1031 *on drighe:* aside
    derely: courteously
1032 *winne:* delightful
    worship: honourable treat-
      ment
    waived: offered, shown
1034 *enbelise:* adorn
    bele: fair
1035 *me worthes the better:* I
    shall be better off
1039 *hest:* command
1042 *fast:* earnestly
1048 *kenely:* daringly
1049 *halet:* gone
1052 *sumned:* summoned
1053 *whiderwarde:* whither
1054 *I nolde bot if I:* I would
    not wish it to happen that
    I should not
1055 *inwith:* within
1056 *enquest:* enquiry
1060 *stabled:* established
    statut: solemn agreement
    steven: appointment
1061 *mere:* appointed place
1062 *bot neked now wontes:* only
    a little (time) now remains
1066 *Naf I:* I have not

Daunced ful drighly with dere caroles.
At the last, when hit was late, thay lachen her leve,
Uchone to wende on his way that was wighe stronge.
Gawain gave him good day, the good mon him laches,
1030 Ledes him to his owen chamber, the chimny beside,
And there he drawes him on drighe, and derely him thonkes
Of the winne worship that he him waived had
As to honour his hous on that high tide
And enbelise his burgh with his bele chere.
1035 "Iwis sir, while I live, me worthes the better
That Gawain has bene my gest at Goddes owen fest."
"Grant merci, sir," quoth Gawain, "in good faith hit is youres,
Al the honour is your owen, the High King you yelde!
And I am wighe at your wille to worche your hest,
1040 As I am holden therto, in high and in lowe,
by right."
The lord fast con him paine
To holde lenger the knight;
To him answares Gawain
1045 By none way that he might.

Then frained the freke ful fair at himselven
What derf dede had him driven at that dere time
So kenely fro the kinges court to cayre al his one
Ere the halidayes holly were halet out of toun.
1050 "For sothe, sir," quoth the segg, "ye sayn bot the trauthe,
A high erand and a hasty me had fro tho wones,
For I am sumned myself to seche to a place
I ne wot in worlde whiderwarde to wende hit to finde.
I nolde bot if I hit negh might on New Yeres morn
1055 For alle the londe inwith Logres, so me oure Lord help.
Forthy, sir, this enquest I require you here,
That ye me telle with trauthe if ever ye tale herde
Of the grene chapel, where hit on grounde stondes,
And of the knight that hit kepes, of colour of grene.
1060 There was stabled by statut a steven us betwene
To meet that mon at that mere, if I might last;
And of that ilk New Yere bot neked now wontes,
And I wolde loke on that lede, if God me let wolde,
Gladloker, by Goddes son, then any good welde!
1065 Forthy, iwis, by your wille, wende me behoves,
Naf I now to busy bot bare thre dayes,

61

1067 *falle feye:* be doomed to die
faily: fail
1069 *terme:* appointed place
1072 *forth dayes:* quite late in the day
1073 *merk:* destination
midmorn: about 9 a.m.
1074 *in spenne:* there (on that ground)
1075 *Dowelles:* stay
1076 *raikes:* depart
1078 *henne:* from here
1079 *gomenly:* merrily
1080 *thrivandely:* heartily
thurgh alle other thinge: (for this) beyond all else
1082 *Dowelle:* stay
elles: in other things
1084 *fette:* brought
1085 *seme:* excellent
1087 *wolde of his wit:* was going out of his mind
1090 *hes:* promise
1092 *bain:* obedient
hest: command
1093 *travailed:* travelled arduously
1094 *warist:* recovered
1096 *loft:* upper room
to-morn while the messewhile: tomorrow morning until breakfast time
1100 *lende:* stay
1104 *Him heldande:* bowing
1106 *worthes to:* will become

And me als fain to falle feye as faily of myn erand."
Then laghande quoth the lord, "Now leng the behoves,
For I shal teche you to that terme by the times ende;
1070 The grene chapel upon grounde greve you no more,
Bot ye shal be in your bed, burn, at thyn ese,
While forth dayes, and ferk on the first of the yere,
And com to that merk at midmorn, to make what you likes
in spenne.
1075   Dowelles while New Yeres day,
And rise, and raikes then,
Mon shal you sette in way,
Hit is not two mile henne."

Then was Gawain ful glad, and gomenly he laghed:
1080 "Now I thonk you thrivandely thurgh alle other thinge;
Now acheved is my chaunce, I shal at your wille
Dowelle, and elles do what ye demen."
Then sesed him the sire and set him beside,
Let the ladies be fette to like him the better.
1085 There was seme solace by hemself stille;
The lord let for luf lotes so mery
As wighe that wolde of his wit, ne wist what he might.
Then he carped to the knight, criande loude,
"Ye han demed to do the dede that I bidde;
1090 Wil ye holde this hes here at this ones?"
"Ye, sir, for sothe," said the segg true,
"While I bide in your burgh, be bain to your hest."
"For ye have travailed," quoth the tulk, "towen fro fer,
And sithen waked me with, ye arn not wel warist
1095 Nauther of sustnaunce ne of slepe, sothly I knowe;
Ye shal lenge in your loft, and lie in your ese
To-morn while the messewhile, and to mete wende
When ye wil, with my wif, that with you shal sitte
And comfort you with companie, til I to court turne;
1100   ye lende,
And I shal erly rise,
On hunting wil I wende."
Gawain grantes alle thise,
Him heldande, as the hende.

1105 "Yet firre," quoth the freke, "a forward we make:
Whatsoever I winne in the wod hit worthes to youres,

1107 *chek:* fortune
therforne: for it
1108 *sware:* answer
1109 *limp:* happens
lere: nothing of value
1110 *grant thertille:* consent to
it
1111 *laike:* amuse yourself
1114 *dalten untightel:* revelled
1115 *while that:* as long as
1116 *Frenkish fare:* French manners, elaborate politeness
1117 *stemmed:* stopped
1119 *light:* gay
1123 *Recorded:* recalled, repeated
1125 *laik:* sport, entertainment
1127 *gromes:* servants
1129 *Tiffen:* prepare
takles: equipment
trussen: pack
males: bags
1130 *Richen hem:* prepare themselves
1135 *sop:* morsel of food
1139 *cacheres:* hunters
couth: could, knew their
craft
coupled: leashed together in
pairs
1141 *motes:* single notes on a
hunting-horn

And what chek so ye acheve chaunge me therforne.
Swete, swap we so, sware with trauthe,
Whether, leude, so limp lere other better."
1110 "By God," quoth Gawain the good, "I grant thertille,
And that you list for to laike, lef hit me thinkes."
"Who bringes us this beverage, this bargain is maked."
So said the lord of that leude; thay laghed uchone,
Thay dronken and dalieden and dalten untightel,
1115 These lordes and ladies, while that hem liked;
And sithen with Frenkish fare and fele fair lotes
Thay stoden and stemmed and stilly speken,
Kisten ful comlily and caghten her leve.
With mony leude ful light and lemande torches
1120 Uche burn to his bed was broght at the last,
　　　　　ful soft.
　　　　To bed yet ere thay yede,
　　　　Recorded covenauntes oft;
　　　　The old lord of that leude
1125　　　Couth well holde laik aloft.

III

Ful erly before the day the folk uprisen,
Gestes that go wolde hor gromes thay calden,
And thay busken up bilive blonkes to sadel,
Tiffen her takles, trussen her males,
1130 Richen hem the richest, to ride alle arayed,
Lepen up lightly, lachen her brideles,
Uche wighe on his way there him wel liked.
The leve lord of the londe was not the last
Arayed for the riding, with renkes ful mony;
1135 Ette a sop hastily, when he had herde masse,
With bugle to bent-felde he buskes bilive.
By that any daylight lemed upon erthe
He with his hatheles on high horses weren.
Then these cacheres that couth coupled hor houndes,
1140 Unclosed the kenel dore and calde hem theroute,
Blew bigly in bugles thre bare motes;

1142 *braches:* hounds
1143 *charred:* sent back
   on chasing that went: those hounds that strayed on other scents
1146 *tristors:* hunting stations
   vewters: keepers of deer-hounds
1147 *couples:* leashes
1149 *rurd:* noise
1150 *quethe:* utterance
   quest: baying of hounds on finding the scent
1151 *doted:* were foolish
1153 *Restayed with:* turned back by
   stablie: ring of beaters
   ascried: shouted
1154 *herttes:* harts
   have the gate: pass freely
1155 *paumes:* "palms", flat parts of horns of deer
1156 *defende:* forbidden
   fermisoun: close season
1157 *meve to:* interfere with
1159 *slades:* valleys

1160 *slipte:* were loosed
   slenting: flight
1161 *wende:* turn
   under wande: in the wood
   wapped: rushed
   flone: arrow
1162 *broun:* brown (skins)
1163 *brayen:* cry out
   dighen: die
1164 *folges:* follow
1166 *crakkande:* echoing
   brusten: burst
1167 *wild:* wild beast
   atwaped: escaped
1168 *toraced:* pulled down
   resait: receiving stations
1169 *tened:* tormented
   taised: harassed
1170 *tristores:* hunting stations
1172 *tofilched:* tore down
1174 *for blisse abloy:* carried away with joy
1178 *laikes:* amuses himself
   eves: edges
1180 *while:* until
   wowes: walls

Braches bayed therfore and breme noise maked;
And thay chastised and charred on chasing that went,
A hundreth of hunteres, as I have herde telle,
1145   of the best.
        To tristors vewters yod,
        Couples huntes of kest;
        There ros for blastes good
        Gret rurd in that forest.

1150 At the first quethe of the quest quaked the wilde;
    Der drof in the dale, doted for drede,
    Highed to the high, bot heterly thay were
    Restayed with the stablie, that stoutly ascried.
    Thay let the herttes have the gate, with the high hedes,
1155 The breme bukkes also with hor brode paumes;
    For the fre lord had defende in fermisoun time
    That there shulde no mon meve to the male der.
    The hindes were holden in with "Hay!" and "Ware!"
    The does driven with gret din to the depe slades.
1160 There might mon se as thay slipte slenting of arwes,
    At uche wende under wande wapped a flone,
    That bigly bot on the broun with ful brode hedes.
    What! Thay brayen and bleden, by bonkes thay dighen,
    And ay raches in a res radly hem folges,
1165 Hunteres with high horne hasted hem after
    With such a crakkande cry as cliffes haden brusten.
    What wild so atwaped wighes that shotten
    Was al toraced and rent at the resait,
    By thay were tened at the high and taised to the wateres;
1170 The leudes were so lerned at the lowe tristores,
    And the grehoundes so gret, that geten hem bilive
And hem tofilched, as fast as frekes might loke,
                there right.
        The lord for blisse abloy
1175   Ful oft con lance and light,
        And drof that day with joy
        Thus to the derk night.

    Thus laikes this lord by linde-wodes eves,
    And Gawain the good mon in gay bed ligges,
1180 Lurkes while the daylight lemed on the wowes,

1181 *covertour:* coverlet
1182 *in slomering he slode:* he slept softly on
sleghly: warily
1186 *waites:* watches
warly: warily
thiderwarde: in that direction
1188 *dernly:* stealthily
1189 *shamed:* was embarrassed
1190 *listily:* cunningly
1191 *stel:* stole
1194 *selly:* exceedingly
1196 *Compast:* pondered
case: occurrence
1197 *Meve (to):* result (in)
1199 *aspye:* discover
spelle: words
in space: soon
1200 *wroth:* stretched himself
to hir warde: towards her
1201 *unlouked:* opened

1202 *sained him:* crossed himself
sawe: prayer
saver: safer
worthe: be made
1205 *in blande:* mingled together
1206 *lete:* speak
1209 *unslighe:* unwary
1210 *astit:* in a moment
true: truce
shape: be arranged
1211 *be ye traist:* be sure
1212 *bourdes:* jests
1214 *Me shal worthe:* it shall be done to me
1215 *yederly:* promptly
yegh after: cry for
1216 *dome:* judgement
nede: of necessity
1217 *bourded:* jested
1219 *deprece:* release
prisoun: prisoner
1221 *kever:* obtain

Under covertour ful clere, cortained aboute;
And as in slomering he slode, sleghly he herde
A little din at his dore, and derfly open;
And he heves up his hed out of the clothes,
1185 A corner of the cortain he caght up a littel
And waites warly thiderwarde what hit be might.
Hit was the lady, loveliest to beholde,
That drow the dore after hir ful dernly and stille
And bowed toward the bed; and the burn shamed,
1190 And laide him doun listily and let as he slepte.
And ho stepped stilly and stel to his bed,
Cast up the cortain and creped withinne,
And set hir ful softly on the bedside,
And lenged there selly long to loke when he wakened.
1195 The leude lay lurked a ful long while,
Compast in his concience to what that case might
Meve other amount; to mervail him thoght;
Bot yet he said in himself, "More semly hit were
To aspye with my spelle in space what ho wolde."
1200 Then he wakened, and wroth, and to hir warde turned,
And unlouked his ighe-liddes, and let as him wondered,
And sained him, as by his sawe the saver to worthe,
           with hande.
      With chin and cheke ful swete,
1205   Both white and red in blande,
      Ful lufly con ho lete
      With lippes smal laghande.

"Good moroun, Sir Gawain," said that gay lady,
"Ye are a sleper unslighe, that mon may slide hider;
1210 Now are ye tan astit! Bot true us may shape
I shal binde you in your bed, that be ye traist."
Al laghande the lady lanced tho bourdes.
"Good moroun, gay," quoth Gawain the blithe,
"Me shal worthe at your wille, and that me wel likes,"
1215 For I yelde me yederly, and yeghe after grace;
And that is the best, by my dome, for me behoves nede."
And thus he bourded again with mony a blithe laghter.
"But wolde ye, lady lovely, then leve me grant,
And deprece your prisoun, and pray him to rise,
1220 I would bowe of this bed, and busk me better,
I shulde kever the more comfort to carp you with."
"Nay, for sothe, beau sir," said that swete,

1223 *rich:* direct
1224 *happe:* clasp, fasten
   half: side
1226 *wene:* know
1227 *worshipes:* honours
1228 *hendelaik:* courtliness
1230 *oure one:* alone
1233 *dit:* locked
1235 *ware:* spend, employ
1237 *cors:* body
1238 *won:* pleasure
   wale: take
1239 *fine force:* sheer necessity
1240 *and shale:* and I will be
1241 *gain:* a good thing
1243 *reche to:* presume to accept
   reherse: describe
1246 *At sawe other at service:* by
   word or deed
1247 *your pris:* you ("your ex-
   cellency")
1250 *lakked:* found fault with
   dainty: courtesy
1251 *that lever were:* whom it
   would delight more
   nowthe: now
1253 *derely:* pleasantly
   dainty: charming
1254 *Kever hem:* obtain
   colen: cool, assuage
1255 *garisoun:* treasure
1256 *lowe:* praise
   lifte: heaven, sky
1261 *skere:* pure
1262 *to uche a case:* to every-
   thing she said

"Ye shal not rise of your bed, I rich you better;
I shal happe you here, that other half als,
1225 And sithen carp with my knight that I caght have.
For I wene wel, iwis, Sir Wawain ye are,
That alle the worlde worshipes whereso ye ride;
Your honour, your hendelaik is hendely praised
With lordes, with ladies, with alle that lif bere;
1230 And now ye are here, iwis, and we bot oure one;
My lord and his leudes are on lenthe faren,
Other burnes in her bed, and my burdes als,
The dore drawen and dit with a derf haspe;
And sithen I have in this hous him that al likes,
1235 I shal ware my while wel while hit lastes,
                    with tale.
            Ye are welcom to my cors,
            Your owen won to wale;
            Me behoves of fine force
1240   Your servaunt be, and shale."

"In good faith," quoth Gawain, "gain hit me thinkes,
Thagh I be not now he that ye of speken;
To reche to such reverence as ye reherse here
I am wighe unworthy, I wot wel myselven.
1245 By God, I were glad, and you good thoght,
At sawe other at service that I sette might
To the plesaunce of your pris, hit were a pure joy."
"In good faith, Sir Gawain," quoth the gay lady,
"The pris and the prowes that pleses al other,
1250 If I hit lakked other set at light, hit were littel dainty;
Bot hit are ladies innowe that lever were nowthe
Have the, hende, in hor holde, as I the habbe here,
To daly with derely your dainty wordes,
Kever hem comfort and colen her cares,
1255 Then much of the garisoun other gold that thay haven.
Bot I lowe that ilk lord that the lifte holdes,
I have hit holly in my hand that al desires,
                    thurgh grace."
            Sho made him so gret chere,
1260   That was so fair of face,
            The knight with speches skere
            Answared to uche a case.

71

1264 *fraunchise:* generosity
1265-1267 "Other people generally copy each other" (im-
plying that the popular
praise of Gawain is merely
a convention); "but the
honour they do me, when
compared with my merits,
is so exaggerated that it
merely makes me look
silly. It is greatly to your
credit that *you* are in-
capable of such unkind-
ness."
1266 *dainty:* honourable treatment
nisen: make foolish by
over-refinement
1267 *worship:* honour
1268 *menskful:* noble (lady)
1269 *won:* multitude
1271 *chepen:* bargain
cheve: gain
1272 *costes:* qualities
1273 *debonerty:* courtesy
semblaunt: manner

1276 *waled:* chosen
1279 *foryelde:* reward
1280 *muchwhat:* many things
midmorn: about 9 a.m.
1282 *feted:* behaved
1284 *in his lode:* with him on his
journey
lur: disaster
soght: was making for
1285 *bout hone:* without delay
1286 *deve:* strike down
1287 *most:* must
1290 *glent:* glance
1291 *stouned:* amazed
stor: strong, hard
1292 *spedes:* blesses
1293 *gos in minde:* is debated in
my mind
1294 *freshly:* quickly
1295 *Ferde:* afraid
castes: speech
1296 *by this skil:* as follows
1297 *gainly:* courteously
1300 *cosse:* kiss
1302 *worthe:* let it be done

"Madame," quoth the mery mon, "Mary you yelde;
For I have founden, in good faith, your fraunchise noble.
1265 And other ful much of other folk fangen hor dedes,
Bot the dainty that thay delen for my desert nisen;
Hit is the worship of yourself, that noght bot wel connes."
"By Mary", quoth the menskful, "me think hit an other;
For were I worth al the won of wimmen alive,
1270 And al the wele of the worlde were in my hand,
And I shulde chepen and chose to cheve me a lord,
For the costes that I have knowen upon the, knight, here,
Of beauty and debonerty and blithe semblaunt,
And that I have ere herkened and holde hit here true,
1275 There shulde no freke upon folde before you be chosen."
"Iwis, worthy," quoth the wighe, "ye have waled wel better;
Bot I am proude of the pris that ye put on me,
And soberly your servaunt, my soverain I holde you
And your knight I becom, and Crist you foryelde."
1280 Thus thay meled of muchwhat til midmorn passed,
And ay the lady let like as him loved much;
The freke ferde with defence, and feted ful fair.
Thagh ho were burde brightest, the burn in minde had
The lasse luf in his lode, for lur that he soght
1285   bout hone,
          The dint that shulde him deve,
          And nedes hit most be done.
          The lady then spek of leve,
          He granted hir ful sone.

1290 Then ho gef him good day, and with a glent laghed,
And as ho stod, ho stouned him with ful stor wordes:
"Now he that spedes uche speche this disport yelde you!
Bot that ye be Gawain, hit gos in minde."
"Wherfore?" quoth the freke, and freshly he askes,
1295 Ferde lest he had failed in forme of his castes;
Bot the burde him blessed, and by this skil said:
"So good as Gawain gainly is holden,
And cortaisie is closed so clene in himselven,
Couth not lightly have lenged so long with a lady
1300 Bot he had craved a cosse, by his cortaisie,
By sum towch of sum trifle at sum tales ende."
Then quoth Wawain, "Iwis, worthe as you likes;
I shal kisse at your comaundement, as a knight falles,
And firre, lest he displease you, so plede hit no more."

1306 *Loutes:* bends
1307 *bekennen:* commend
1309 *dos hir:* goes
1309 *riches him:* prepares himself
rapes: hastens
1310 *Clepes:* calls
1311 *boun:* ready
1312 *menskly:* worthily
kepes: occupies
1313 *mone:* moon
1316 *digne:* worthy
1318 *solace set:* made merry
same: together
1319 *is lent:* has gone
1320 *holtes:* woods
hethe: heath
1321 *sowme:* number
slowe: slew
heldet: sank
1322 *deme:* tell
1323 *fersly:* proudly
1324 *quelled:* killed
querry: heap
1326 *grattest of grece:* fattest
1327 *didden hem undo:* had them
cut open
derely: neatly.
1328 *assay:* a cut made through
the deer's skin and flesh
to judge the quality and
quantity of the venison

1329 *fingeres:* fingers' breadth
foulest: poorest in quality
1330 *slot:* hollow above breast-
bone at base of throat
erber: first stomach
1331 *Shaved:* cut away
knitten: tied, sewed
1332 *ritte:* cut
1334 *Listily:* skilfully
forlancing: throwing out
lere: flesh
knot: a piece of flesh between the neck and shoul-
der
1335 *gargulun:* throat
departed: separated
1336 *wesaunt:* oesophagus
walt: tossed
1337 *sher:* cut
1338 *Haled:* drew
1339 *brittened:* chopped up
1340 *gargulun:* throat
1341 *Rives:* cuts
bight: fork of legs
1342 *Voides out:* clears out
avanters: part of the offal
1344 *ridde of:* clear away
rigge: back
1345 *Evenden:* straight down
1346 *heven:* lift

1305 Ho comes nerre with that, and caches him in armes,
Loutes luflich adoun and the leude kisses.
Thay comly bekennen to Crist aither other;
Ho dos hir forth at the dore withouten din more;
And he riches him to rise and rapes him sone,
1310 Clepes to his chamberlain, choses his wede,
Bowes forth, when he was boun, blithely to masse;
And then he meved to his mete that menskly him keped,
And made mery all day til the mone rised,
                    with game.
1315   Was never freke fairer fonge
                Betwene two so digne dame,
                The alder and the yonge;
                Much solace set thay same.

And ay the lord of the londe is lent on his games,
1320 To hunt in holtes and hethe at hindes baraine.
Such a sowme he there slowe by that the sunne heldet,
Of dos and of other der, to deme were wonder.
Then fersly thay flokked in folk at the last,
And quikly of the quelled der a querry thay maked.
1325 The best bowed therto with burnes innowe,
Gedered the grattest of grece that there were,
And didden hem derely undo as the dede askes;
Serched hem at the assay sum that there were,
Two fingeres thay founde of the foulest of alle.
1330 Sithen thay slit the slot, sesed the erber,
Shaved with a sharp knif, and the shire knitten;
Sithen ritte thay the foure limmes, and rent of the hide,
Then brek thay the baly, the boweles out token,
Listily forlancing, and lere of the knot;
1335 Thay gripped to the gargulun, and graithely departed
The wesaunt fro the wind-hole, and walt out the guttes;
Then sher thay out the shulderes with her sharp knives,
Haled hem by a littel hole to have hole sides.
Sithen brittened thay the brest and braiden hit in twaine,
1340 And eft at the gargulun begines one then,
Rives hit up radly right to the bight,
Voides out the avanters, and veraily therafter
Alle the rimes by the ribbes radly thay lance;
So ridde thay of by resoun by the rigge bones,
1345 Evenden to the haunche, that henged alle samen,
And heven hit up al hole, and hewen hit of there,

1347 *neme for:* took to be
noumbles: offal
1349 *bight:* fork
1350 *lappes:* folds of skin
1352 *unbinde:* cut in two
1355 *corbeles:* raven's
1356 *thurled:* made a hole in
1357 *hoghes:* hocks
fourches: legs
1360 *lightes:* lights, lungs
lether of the paunches: tripe
1361 *blende:* mixed
theramonges: with it
1362 *pris:* blast on horn when
animal is caught
1363 *folden:* turn, go
1364 *strakende:* sounding
motes: single notes on
hunting horn
1365 *was wonnen:* had arrived
1368 *bette:* kindled
1369 *thertille:* to it
1372 *samen:* assemble
1377 *tailes:* tallies, notched sticks
showing number of deer
killed
tait: nimble
1378 *grece:* fat and flesh
shorne: cut
1379 *payes:* pleases
pris: praise
1380 *thrivandely:* abundantly
served: deserved
1381 *wayth:* meat obtained by
hunting
1387 *worthes to:* shall be

And that thay neme for the noumbles by name, as I trowe,
              by kinde;
      By the bight al of the thighes
1350   The lappes thay lance behinde;
      To hewe hit in two thay highes,
      By the bakbon to unbinde.

Both the hed and the hals thay hewen of then,
And sithen sunder thay the sides swift fro the chine,
1355 And the corbeles fee thay cast in a greve;
Then thurled thay aither thik side thurgh by the ribbe,
And henged then aither by hoghes of the fourches,
Uche freke for his fee, as falles for to have.
Upon a felle of the fair best fede thay thair houndes
1360 With the liver and the lightes, the lether of the paunches,
And bred bathed in blod blende theramonges.
Boldly thay blew pris, bayed thair raches,
Sithen fange thay her flesh, folden to home,
Strakande ful stoutly mony stif motes.
1365 By that the daylight was done the douth was al wonnen
Into the comly castel, there the knight bides
              ful stille,
      With blisse and bright fire bette;
      The lord is comen thertille;
1370   When Gawain with him mette
      There was bot wele at wille.

Then comaunded the lord in that sale to samen alle the meiny,
Both the ladies on lowe to light with her burdes;
Before alle the folk on the flet frekes he biddes
1375 Veraily his venisoun to fech him beforne,
And al goodly in gamen Gawain he called,
Teches him to the tailes of ful tait bestes,
Shewes him the shire grece shorne upon ribbes.
"How payes you this play?   Have I pris wonnen?
1380 Have I thrivandely thonk thurgh my craft served?"
"Ye iwis," quoth that other wighe, "here is wayth fairest
That I segh this seven yere in sesoun of winter."
"And al I give you, Gawain," quoth the gome then,
"For by accorde of covenaunt ye crave hit as your owen."
1385 "This is sothe," quoth the segg, "I say you that ilke:
That I have worthily wonnen these wones withinne
Iwis with as good wille hit worthes to youres."

1389 *avise:* devise, contrive
1390 *chevisaunce:* winnings
    cheved: obtained
1391 *I vouche hit saf:* I would
    freely grant it
    finely: completely
1393 *breve:* declare
1396 *you tides:* is due to you
1399 *to lowe:* praiseworthy
1400 *soper:* supper
    as-swithe: at once
1403 *wale:* choice
    weghed: brought
1404 *bourding:* jesting
1405 *fille:* fulfil
1406 *chevisaunce:* winnings
1407 *what newes:* whatever new
    thing
    nome: obtained
1408 *accorded of:* agreed to
1409 *bourde:* jest
1413 *lopen:* leapt
1414 *metely:* duly
    delivered: dealt with,
    finished
1415 *dressed:* went
    sprenged: broke
1418 *in space:* soon after
1420 *on race:* headlong
1421 *calle of:* call for
    quest: search for game
    in a kerre side: beside a
    marsh
1422 *rehaited:* encouraged
    minged: announced
1423 *warp:* uttered
    wrast: loud
1424 *swithe:* quickly
1425 *fuyt:* trail
1426 *glaver:* uproar
    glam: din
1427 *rocheres:* rocks
1428 *hardened:* encouraged

He haspes his fair hals his armes withinne
And kisses him as comlily as he couth avise;
1390 "Tas you there my chevisaunce, I cheved no more;
I vouche hit saf finely, thagh feler hit were."
"Hit is good," quoth the good mon, "grant merci therfore.
Hit may be such, hit is the better, and ye me breve wolde
Where ye wan this ilk wele by wit of yourselven."
1395 "That was not forward," quoth he, "fraist me no more,
For ye have tan that you tides, trowe ye none other
        ye mowe."
        Thay laghed, and made hem blithe
        With lotes that were to lowe;
1400   To soper thay yede as-swithe,
        With dainties newe innowe.

And sithen by the chimny in chamber thay seten,
Wighes the wale wine weghed to hem oft,
And eft in her bourding thay baithen in the morn
1405 To fille the same forwardes that thay before maden:
What chaunce so betides hor chevisaunce to chaunge,
What newes so thay nome, at night when thay metten.
Thay accorded of the covenauntes before the court alle;
The beverage was broght forth in bourde at that time,
1410 Then thay lovelich leghten leve at the last,
Uche burn to his bed busked bilive.
By that the cok had crowen and cakled bot thrise
The lord was lopen of his bed, the leudes uchone;
So that the mete and the masse was metely delivered,
1415 The douth dressed to the wod, ere any day sprenged,
        to chace;
        High with hunte and hornes
        Thurgh plaines thay passe in space,
        Uncoupled among tho thornes
1420   Raches that ran on race.

Sone thay calle of a quest in a kerre side,
The hunte rehaited the houndes that hit first minged,
Wilde wordes him warp with a wrast noise;
The houndes that hit herde hasted thider swithe,
1425 And fellen as fast to the fuyt, fourty at ones;
Then such a glaver and glam of gedered raches
Ros, that the rocheres rungen aboute;
Hunteres hem hardened with horne and with mouth.

1429 *sembly:* crowd
sweyed: rushed
1430 *floshe:* pool
frith: wood
foo: forbidding
1431 *at the kerre side:* beside the marsh
1432 *rocher:* rock
unridely: untidily
1434 *umbecasten:* searched about
knarre: gnarled rock
1435 *while:* until
1436 *best:* beast
breved was with: was announced by
1437 *buskes:* bushes
1438 *unsoundily:* disastrously
soght: made for, rushed at
overthwert: in his way
1439 *sellokest:* most marvellous, most huge
swenged: rushed
1140 *sounder:* herd
wight: creature
forolde: had grown old
1441 *bor:* boar
alder grattest: biggest of all
1442 *gronied:* grunted
1443 *thrast:* thrust (noun)
thright: thrust (verb, past tense)
1444 *sparred:* sprang
bout: without
spit: doing harm

1446 *rechated:* blew the "recall", indicating where the hunters should assemble
1449 *quelle:* kill
1451 *maimes:* injures
mute: pack of hounds
in melle: on all sides
1453 *yomerly:* piteously
1455 *Haled:* loosed (from bow)
1456 *paired at:* were impaired by
pith: toughness
pight: struck
sheldes: tough skin and flesh at the shoulders
1457 *brawne:* flesh
1458 *shaven:* smooth
shindered: broke, was shattered
1459 *hipped again:* bounced off
1460 *dered:* hurt
drighe: hard
1461 *brainwode:* mad
bate: fighting
rases: rushes
1463 *arghed:* were terrified
on lite: back
1466 *rechated:* blew the recall (see note on l. 1446)
rones: bushes
1467 *Suande:* following
shafted: set

Then al in a sembly sweyed togeder
1430 Betwene a floshe in that frith and a foo cragge;
In a knot by a cliff, at the kerre side,
There as the rugh rocher unridely was fallen,
Thay ferden to the finding, and frekes hem after;
Thay umbecasten the knarre and the knot both,
1435 Wighes, while thay wisten wel withinne hem hit were,
The best that there breved was with the blodhoundes.
Then thay beten on the buskes, and bede him uprise,
And he unsoundily out soght segges overthwert;
One the sellokest swin swenged out there,
1440 Long sithen fro the sounder that wight forolde.
For he was breme, bor alder grattest;
Ful grimme when he gronied, then greved mony,
For thre at the first thrast he thright to the erthe,
And sparred forth good speed bout spit more.
1445 These other halowed "High!" ful high, and "Hay, hay!" cried,
Haden hornes to mouth, heterly rechated;
Mony was the mery mouth of men and of houndes
That buskes after this bor with bost and with noise
                    to quelle.
1450   Ful oft he bides the bay,
             And maimes the mute in melle;
             He hurtes of the houndes, and thay
             Ful yomerly yaule and yelle.

Shalkes to shote at him showven to then,
1455 Haled to him of her arwes, hitten him oft;
Bot the pointes paired at the pith that pight in his sheldes,
And the barbes of his brawne bite none wolde
Thagh the shaven shaft shindered in peces;
The hed hipped again wheresoever hit hitte.
1460 Bot when the dintes him dered of her drighe strokes,
Then, brainwode for bate, on burnes he rases,
Hurtes hem ful heterly there he forth highes,
And mony arghed therat, and on lite drowen.
Bot the lord on a light horse lances him after,
1465 As burn bold upon bent his bugle he blowes,
He rechated, and rode thurgh rones ful thik,
Suande this wilde swin til the sunne shafted.
This day with this ilk dede thay driven on this wise,
While oure luflich leude lies in his bed,

1470 *geres:* bedclothes
1473 *salue:* greet, wish good-morning
1475 *mode:* heart, mood
remue: alter
1476 *totes:* peeps
1478 *yeldes:* answers
yern: eagerly
1479 *swithely:* very much
1480 *loke:* look
1482 *wrast:* disposed
1483 *companie:* polite society
costes: manners
1484 *kennes:* teaches
1485 *yederly:* promptly
1486 *alder truest:* truest of all
1488 *breve:* declare
1489 *kende:* taught
1490 *countenaunce is couth:* favour is evident
1492 *Do way . . . that speche:* say no more of that
1494 *werned:* refused
1495 *Ma fay:* by my faith
1497 *vilanous:* ill-bred
devaye: deny, refuse
1499 *unthrivande:* unprofitable
thede: land
lende: come from
1503 *in space:* soon
1504 *loutes:* bends
1507 *druries greme and grace:* love's sorrows and delights
1508 *wit at:* learn from
1509 *wrathed not:* were not angry
skil: reason
1510 *yepe:* active
1511 *oute:* far and wide

1470 Gawain graithely at home, in geres ful rich
                    of hue.
              The lady noght forgate
              Com to him to salue;
              Ful erly ho was him at
1475   His mode for to remue.

    Ho comes to the cortain, and at the knight totes;
    Sir Wawain hir welcomed worthy on first,
    And ho him yeldes again ful yern of hir wordes,
    Settes hir softly by his side, and swithely ho laghes,
1480 And with a lufllich loke ho laide him these wordes:
    "Sir, if ye be Wawain, wonder me thinkes,
    Wighe that is so wel wrast alway to good,
    And connes not of companie the costes undertake,
    And if mon kennes you hom to knowe, ye cast hom of your minde;
1485 Thou has forgeten yederly that yisterday I taghte
    By alder truest token of talk that I couth."
    "What is that?" quoth the wighe, "Iwis I wot never;
    If hit be sothe that ye breve, the blame is myn owen."
    "Yet I kende you of kissing," quoth the clere then,
1490 "Whereso countenaunce is couth quikly to claime;
    That becomes uche a knight that cortaisie uses."
    "Do way," quoth that derf mon, "my dere, that speche,
    For that durst I not do, lest I denayed were;
    If I were werned, I were wrang, iwis, if I profered."
1495 "Ma fay," quoth the mery wif, "ye may not be werned,
    Ye are stif innowe to constraine with strenthe, if you likes,
    If any were so vilanous that you devaye wolde."
    "Ye, by God," quoth Gawain, "good is your speche,
    Bot threte is unthrivande in thede there I lende,
1500 And uche gift that is geven not with good wille.
    I am at your comaundement, to kisse when you likes,
    Ye may lach when you list, and leve when you thinkes,
                    in space."
              The lady loutes adoun
1505   And comlily kisses his face;
              Much speche thay there expoun
              Of druries greme and grace.

    "I wolde wit at you, wighe," that worthy there said,
    "And you wrathed not therwith, what were the skil
1510 That so yong and so yepe as ye at this time,
    So cortais, so knightly, as ye are knowen oute,

                          83

1512 *alosed:* praised
1513 *laik:* sport
lettrure: science
1514 *teveling:* labour, deeds
1515 *titelet token:* main theme
tixt: text
1516 *auntered:* adventured
1517 *doelful stoundes:* grievous
times
1518 *venged:* avenged themselves
voided: got rid of
1519 *boure:* lady's bower (bedroom)
1520 *comlokest:* most handsome
kidde: reputed
elde: age, generation
1521 *word:* fame
walkes: are spread about
1522 *sere twies:* on two separate
occasions
1523 *helde:* come
1524 *longed:* belonged
1525 *hetes:* vows (of knightly
service)
1526 *Oghe:* ought
yern: eagerly

1528 *lewed:* ignorant
los: fame
1529 *Other elles:* or else
to dille: too stupid, too dull
1531 *sengel:* alone
1535 *foryelde:* reward
1537 *winne:* come
1538 *pine you:* trouble yourself
1539 *anyskinnes:* any kind of
countenaunce: favour
keveres: gives
1540 *torvaile:* hard task
1541 *towche:* deal with
temes: themes
tixt: romance, stories
1542 *sleght:* skill
1543 *or:* than
1544 *erde:* land
1545 *felefolde:* manifold, mul-
tiple
1546 *wilning:* desire
at my might: as far as I can
1549 *fondet:* tempted
1550 *woghe:* wrong, sin
1551 *semed:* was seen

And of alle chevalry to chose, the chef thing alosed
Is the lel laik of luf, the lettrure of armes;
For to telle of this teveling of these true knightes
1515 Hit is the titelet token, and tixt of her werkes
How leudes for her lel luf hor lives han auntered,
Endured for her drury doelful stoundes,
And after venged with valour and voided her care
And broght blisse into boure with bounties hor owen;
1520 And ye are knight comlokest kidde of your elde,
Your word and your worship walkes aywhere,
And I have seten by yourself here sere twies,
Yet herde I never of your hed helde no wordes
That ever longed to luf, lasse ne more;
1525 And ye, that are so cortais and quaint of your hetes,
Oghe to a yong thing yern to shewe
And teche sum tokenes of trueluf craftes.
Why, are ye lewed that alle the los weldes?
Other elles ye demen me to dille your daliaunce to herken?
1530   For shame!
          I com hider sengel, and sitte
          To lerne at you sum game;
          Dos, teches me of your wit
          While my lord is fro hame."

1535 "In good faith," quoth Gawain, "God you foryelde!
Gret is the good gle, and gamen to me huge,
That so worthy as ye wolde winne hider
And pine you with so pore a mon, as play with your knight
With anyskinnes countenaunce, hit keveres me ese.
1540 Bot to take the torvaile to myself to trueluf expoun
And towche the temes of tixt and tales of armes
To you that, I wot wel, weldes more sleght
Of that art, by the half, or a hundreth of such
As I am, other ever shal, in erde there I live,
1545 Hit were a foly felefolde, my fre, by my trauthe.
I wolde your wilning worche at my might,
As I am highly beholden, and evermore wille
Be servaunt to yourselven, so save me Drightin!"
Thus him frained that fre, and fondet him oft
1550 For to have wonnen him to woghe, whatso sho thoght elles;
Bot he defended him so fair that no faut semed,
Ne non evel on nauther half, nauther thay wisten
          bot blisse.

1554 *laiked:* played
1558 *ruthes him:* bestirs himself
1559 *dight:* prepared
    derely: splendidly
1560 *laiked:* played
1562 *Sues:* follows
    uncely: ill-fated, wretched
    swinges: rushes
1563 *braches:* hounds
1565 *maugref his hed:* against his will, in spite of his efforts
    utter: out, into the open
1566 *flones:* arrows
    flet: flew
1567 *by stoundes:* at times
1568 *mate:* exhausted
1569 *winnes:* reaches
1570 *rasse:* smooth bank
    borne: stream
1571 *scrape:* sharpen his tusks by striking the upper and lower ones together
1572 *femed:* foamed
    unfair: hideous
    wikes: corners
1573 *tushes:* tusks

1573-75 *irked . . . to nye him on-ferum:* grew tired of attacking him from a distance
1576 *wothe:* danger
1578 *lothe:* hateful
1579 *tushes:* tusks
1580 *brainwode:* frenzied
1581 *cachande:* urging on
1583 *corsour:* horse
1585 *Foundes:* hastens
    felle: wild beast
1586 *wilde:* wild beast
    was war of: saw
1587 *Hef . . . the here:* raised his bristles
    fnast: snorted, panted
1588 *ferde:* feared
    worre: worst of it
1589 *settes him out on:* rushes out at
1591 *wightest:* most fierce
    worre: worst of it
1593 *Sadly:* firmly
    slot: hollow above breast-bone at base of throat
1594 *hult:* hilt
    shindered: burst asunder

Thay laghed and laiked long,
At the last sho con him kisse;
Hir leve fair con sho fonge
And went hir way, iwis.

Then ruthes him the renk and rises to the masse,
And sithen hor diner was dight and derely served.
The leude with the ladies laiked alle day,
Bot the lord over the londes lanced ful oft,
Sues his uncely swin, that swinges by the bonkes
And bote the best of his braches the bakkes in sunder
There he bode in his bay, til bawemen hit breken,
And made him maugref his hed for to meve utter,
So fele flones there flet when the folk gedered.
Bot yet the stiffest to start by stoundes he made,
Til at the last he was so mate he might no more renne,
Bot in the haste that he might he to a hole winnes
Of a rasse by a rokke there rennes the borne.
He gete the bonk at his bak, begines to scrape,
The frothe femed at his mouth unfair by the wikes,
Whettes his white tushes; with him then irked
Alle the burnes so bold that him by stoden
To nye him on-ferum, bot neghe him none durst
          for wothe;
          He had hurt so mony beforne
          That al thoght then ful lothe
          Be more with his tushes torne,
          That breme was and brainwode both;

Til the knight com himself, cachande his blonk,
Segh him bide at the bay, his burnes beside.
He lightes luflich adoun, leves his corsour,
Braides out a bright bronde and bigly forth strides,
Foundes fast thurgh the forde there the felle bides.
The wilde was ware of the wighe with weppen in hand,
Hef highly the here, so heterly he fnast
That fele ferde for the freke, lest felle him the worre.
The swin settes him out on the segg even,
That the burn and the bor were both upon hepes
In the wightest of the water; the worre had that other,
For the mon merkes him wel, as thay mette first,
Set sadly the sharp in the slot even,
Hit him up to the hult, that the hert shindered,

1595 *yarrande:* snarling
1596 *tite:* quickly
1600 *to dethe endite:* kill
1601 *pris:* blast on horn when
    animal is caught
1603 *Brachetes:* hounds
1604 *chargeaunt:* arduous
1606 *unlace:* cut up
1608 *rigge:* back
1609 *glede:* red-hot coal
1610 *blent:* mixed
    braches: hounds
1611 *brittenes:* cuts
    brawne: flesh
    sheldes: slabs
1612 *hastlettes:* edible entrails
    hightly: fitly
1613 *halches:* fastens
1614 *stange:* pole
1615 *swengen:* hasten
1617 *forferde:* killed
1620 *him thoght ful long:* he was
    impatient
1621 *gain:* promptly
1626 *sheldes:* slabs of boar's flesh
    shapes: gives
1627 *largesse:* great size
    lithernes: ferocity
1628 *werre:* fighting
1631 *such a brawne of a best:* so
    much flesh on any boar
1634 *let lodly:* expressed horror
    here: praise

1595 And he yarrande him yelde, and yed over the water
                   ful tite.
          A hundreth houndes him hent
          That bremely con him bite,
          Burnes him broght to bent
1600   And dogges to dethe endite.

There was blawing of pris in mony breme horne,
High halowing on high with hatheles that might;
Brachetes bayed that best, as bidden the maisteres
Of that chargeaunt chace that were chef huntes.
1605 Then a wighe that was wis upon wodcraftes
To unlace this bor lufly begines.
First he hewes of his hed and on high settes,
And sithen rendes him al rugh by the rigge after,
Braides out the boweles, brennes hom on glede,
1610 With bred blent therwith his braches rewardes.
Sithen he brittenes out the brawne in bright brode sheldes,
And has out the hastlettes, as hightly besemes;
And yet hem halches al hole the halves togeder,
And sithen on a stif stange stoutly hem henges.
1615 Now with this ilk swin thay swengen to home;
The bores hed was borne before the burnes selven
That him forferde in the forde thurgh force of his hand
                so stronge;
          Til he segh Sir Gawain
1620   In halle him thoght ful long;
          He calde, and he com gain
          His fees there for to fonge.

The lord ful loude with lote laghed mery
When he segh Sir Gawain, with solace he spekes;
1625 The good ladies were geten, and gedered the meiny;
He shewes hem the sheldes, and shapes hem the tale
Of the largesse and the lenthe, the lithernes als
Of the werre of the wilde swin in wod there he fled.
That other knight ful comly comended his dedes
1630 And praised hit as gret pris that he proved had,
For such a brawne of a best, the bold burn said,
Ne such sides of a swin segh he never ere.
Then handeled thay the huge hed; the hende mon hit praised,
And let lodly therat the lord for to here.
1635 "Now, Gawain," quoth the good mon, "this gamen is your owen

1638 *Alle my get:* all that I get
1640 *eftersones:* again immediately afterwards
1642 *knit:* make fast
1644 *Gile:* Giles
1647 *chaffer:* trade, bargain
1648 *telded:* set up
trestes: trestles
1650 *by wowes:* on the walls
1652 *glam:* noise of merry-making
glent: sprang
1653 *on fele wise:* in many ways
1654 *soper:* supper
athel: splendid
1655 *coundutes:* carols
caroles: dances accompanied with song
1656 *manerly:* seemly
1658 *semblaunt:* expression
1659 *stollen:* stealthy
countenaunce: look of favour

1660 *forwondered:* astonished
wroth: angry
1661 *nurture:* good breeding
nurne hir againes: respond to her advances
1662 *dainty:* courtesy
turned towrast: might lead to difficulties
1669 *nurne on the same note:* propose the same terms
1671 *terme:* appointment
to shulde: must go to
1672 *letted:* dissuaded
to lenge him restayed: persuaded him to stay
1673 *siker my trauthe:* give my word
1674 *cheve to:* reach
charres: affairs
1675 *prime:* the first part of the day (6 to 9 a.m.)
1676 *loft:* bedroom

By fine forwarde and faste, faithely ye knowe."
"Hit is sothe," quoth the segg, "and as siker true
Alle my get I shal you give again, by my trauthe."
He hent the hathel aboute the hals, and hendely him kisses,
1640 And eftersones of the same he served him there.
"Now are we even," quoth the hathel, "in this eventide
Of alle the convenauntes that we knit, sithen I com hider,
        by lawe."
      The lord said, "By Saint Gile,
1645   Ye are the best that I knowe!
      Ye ben rich in a while,
      Such chaffer and ye drowe."

Then thay telded tables trestes aloft,
Casten clothes upon; clere light then
1650 Wakened by wowes, waxen torches;
Segges sette and served in sale al aboute;
Much glam and gle glent up therinne
Aboute the fire upon flet, and on fele wise
At the soper and after, mony athel songes,
1655 As coundutes of Cristemas and caroles newe,
With al the manerly mirthe that mon may of telle,
And ever oure luflich knight the lady beside.
Such semblaunt to that segg semly ho made
With stille stollen countenaunce, that stalworth to plese,
1660 That al forwondered was the wighe, and wroth with himselven,
Bot he nolde for his nurture nurne hir againes,
Bot dalt with hir al in dainty, howsoever the dede turned
        towrast.
      When thay had played in halle
1665   As long as hor wille hom last,
      To chamber he con him calle,
      And to the chimny thay past.

And there thay dronken, and dalten, and demed eft newe
To nurne on the same note on New Yeres even;
1670 Bot the knight craved leve to cayre on the morn,
For hit was negh at the terme that he to shulde.
The lord him letted of that, to lenge him restayed,
And said, "As I am true segg, I siker my trauthe
Thou shal cheve to the grene chapel thy charres to make,
1675 Leude, on New Yeres light, long before prime.
Forthy thou lie in thy loft and lach thyn ese,

1677 *towches:* terms of the agreement
1678 *chevisaunce:* winnings
charre: return
1680 *thrid time throwe best:* may the third time turn out best
1681 *minne upon:* give our minds to
1682 *lur:* sorrow
1683 *lenged:* persuaded to stay
1688 *kepes:* attends to
1689 *dight:* ready
1691 *mounture:* horse
1692 *helden:* go
1693 *boun:* ready
1694 *Ferly:* wonderfully
forst: frost
clenged: clung
1695 *rudede:* reddened, fiery
rak: drifting clouds
1696 *costes:* passes by the side of
welkin: sky
1697 *unhardeled:* unleashed hounds
holt: wood
1698 *Rocheres:* rocks
by ris: in the woods
1699 *fuyt:* trail
1700 *a traveres:* across
traunt: cunning practice

1701 *kenet:* small dog
cries therof: gives tongue at it (the line of scent)
1702 *felaghes:* companions
fnasted: panted
1703 *fare:* track
1704 *fiskes:* scampers
1705 *sued:* followed
1706 *Wreghande:* denouncing
weterly: clearly
wroth: fierce
1707 *trantes:* dodges
tornayes: doubles back
tene: troublesome
1708 *Havilounes:* dodges back
hegges: hedges
1709 *spenny:* spinney, cluster of bushes
1710 *strothe rande:* edge of a small wood
1711 *Wende have wilt:* thought he might escape
1712 *wale:* excellent
tristor: hunting-station
1713 *thro:* fierce ones
thrich: rush
thrat: attacked
1715 *blenched:* started aside
1716 *on stray:* in a different direction

And I shal hunt in this holt, and holde the towches,
Chaunge with the chevisaunce, by that I charre hider;
For I have fraisted the twies, and faithful I finde the;
1680 Now, thrid time throwe best; thenk on the morne,
Make we mery while we may and minne upon joy,
For the lur may mon lach whenso mon likes."
This was graithely granted, and Gawain is lenged;
Blithe broght was him drink, and thay to bed yeden
1685   with light.
      Sir Gawain lies and slepes
      Ful stille and soft al night;
      The lord that his craftes kepes
      Ful erly he was dight.

1690 After masse a morsel he and his men token;
Mery was the morning, his mounture he askes.
Alle the hatheles that on horse shulde helden him after
Were boun busked on hor blonkes before the halle gates.
Ferly fair was the folde, for the forst clenged;
1695 In red rudede upon rak rises the sunne,
And ful clere costes the cloudes of the welkin.
Hunteres unhardeled by a holt side,
Rocheres rungen by ris for rurd of her hornes;
Sum fel in the fuyt there the fox bade,
1700 Trailes oft a traveres by traunt of her wiles;
A kenet cries thereof, the hunte on him calles;
His felaghes fallen him to, that fnasted ful thik,
Runnen forth in a rabel in his right fare,
And he fiskes hem before; thay founden him sone,
1705 And when thay seghe him with sight thay sued him fast,
Wreghande him ful weterly with a wroth noise;
And he trantes and tornayes thurgh mony tene greve,
Havilounes, and herkenes by hegges ful ofte.
At the last by a littel dich he lepes over a spenny,
1710 Steles out ful stilly by a strothe rande,
Wende have wilt of the wod with wiles fro the houndes;
Then was he went ere he wist to a wale tristor,
There thre thro at a thrich thrat him at ones,
          al gray.
1715   He blenched again bilive
      And stifly start on stray;
      With alle the wo on live
      To the wod he went away.

1719 *lif upon list:* excellent sport
     lithen: hear
1720 *mute:* pack of hounds
     menged: crowded
1721 *sette:* called down
1722 *clamberande:* clustering
1724 *yained:* greeted
     yarrande: chiding
1725 *threted:* reviled
1726 *titleres:* ticklers (the hounds
     close behind him)
1727 *out raiked:* made for the
     open
1728 *reled:* turned suddenly
1729 *ye he lad hem by lagmon:*
     indeed, he led them astray
1730 *mid over-under:* midday
1734 *paire:* fail
     pight: was fixed
1735 *raiked hir:* went
1736 *mete:* extending
1737 *pured:* trimmed
1738 *hagher:* well-wrought
1739 *Trased:* twined
     tressour: head-dress
1740 *thriven:* fair
1744 *rehayted:* rebuked
1750 *drighe:* heavy, deep
     draveled: muttered in his
     sleep
1751 *thro:* oppressive
1752 *wirde:* fate
1754 *debate:* resistance
1755 *kevered:* recovered
1756 *Swenges:* comes suddenly
     swevenes: dreams
     swares: answers
1758 *fetly:* daintily
1759 *wale:* excellent

Then was hit lif upon list to lithen the houndes,
1720 When alle the mute had him met, menged togeder.
Such a sorewe at that sight thay sette on his hed
As alle the clamberande cliffes had clatered on hepes;
Here he was halowed, when hatheles him metten,
Loude he was yained with yarrande speche;
1725 There he was threted and oft thef called,
And ay the titleres at his tail, that tary he ne might;
Oft he was runnen at, when he out raiked,
And oft reled in again, so Reynarde was wily.
And ye he lad hem by lagmon, the lord and his meiny,
1730 On this maner by the mountes while mid over-under,
While the hende knight at home holsumly slepes
Withinne the comly cortaines, on the colde morn.
Bot the lady for luf let not to slepe,
Ne the purpose to paire that pight in hir hert,
1735 Bot ros hir up radly, raiked hir theder
In a mery mantile, mete to the erthe,
That was furred ful fine with felles wel pured,
No hues good on hir hed bot the hagher stones
Trased aboute hir tressour by twenty in clusteres;
1740 Hir thriven face and hir throte throwen al naked,
Hir brest bare before and behinde eke.
Ho comes withinne the chamber dore and closes hit hir after,
Waives up a window, and on the wighe calles
And radly thus rehayted him with hir rich wordes,
1745   with chere:
          "A, mon, how may thou slepe?
          This morning is so clere!"
          He was in drouping depe,
          Bot then he con hir here.

1750 In drighe drouping of dreme draveled that noble,
As mon that was in mourning of mony thro thoghtes,
How that destiny shulde that day dele him his wirde
At the grene chapel, when he the gome metes,
And behoves his buffet abide withoute debate more;
1755 Bot when that comly com he kevered his wittes,
Swenges out of the swevenes, and swares with hast.
The lady luflich com laghande swete,
Felle over his fair face, and fetly him kissed;
He welcomes hir worthily with a wale chere.
1760 He segh hir so glorious and gaily atired,

95

1761 *fetures:* parts (of body)
1762 *Wight:* ardently
wallande: welling up
1763 *smoth:* courteous
smolt: gentle
smeten into mirthe: at once started joking
1764 *bonchef:* happiness
breke: was spoken
1765 *winne:* joy
1769 *Nif:* if not
minne: had taken care
1770 *princece:* princess
depresed: attacked, besieged
1771 *Nurned:* urged
negh the thred: near the limit
nede: necessarily
1772 *lodly:* offensive
1773 *crathain:* villain
1774 *his mischef:* the disaster to himself
1775 *telde:* house
aght: owned
1776 *God shilde:* God forbid

1777 *lite:* little
1778 *specialty:* partiality, fondness
1780 *lif:* person
1782 *lemman:* mistress
lever: dearer one
1783 *folden:* pledged
festned: bound
1784 *lausen:* break
leve: believe
nowthe: now
1786 *upon live:* on earth
laine: conceal
1789 *smethely:* gently
1792 *that wight:* she
1793 *swared:* answered
1794 *cach:* hasten
hethen: away
1795 *upon molde:* while I live
may: woman
1796 *Sikande:* sighing
sweghe: stooped
1797 *severes:* departs
1800 *minne on:* be reminded of
lassen: lessen

So fautles of hir fetures and of so fine hues,
Wight wallande joy warmed his hert.
With smothe smiling and smolt thay smeten into mirthe,
That al was blisse and bonchef that breke him betwene,
1765   and winne.
        Thay lanced wordes good,
        Much wele then was therinne;
        Gret peril betwene hem stod,
        Nif Mary of hir knight minne.

1770 For that princece of pris depresed him so thik,
Nurned him so negh the thred, that nede him behoved
Other lach there hir luf, other lodly refuse.
He cared for his cortaisie, lest crathain he were,
And more for his meschef, if he shulde make sinne
1775 And be traitor to that tulk that that telde aght.
"God shilde," quoth the shalk, "that shal not befalle!"
With luf-laghing a lite he laid him beside
Alle the speches of specialty that sprange of hir mouthe.
Quoth that burde to that burn, "Blame ye deserve
1780 If ye luf not that lif that ye lie nexte,
Before alle the wighes in the worlde wounded in hert,
Bot if ye have a lemman, a lever, that you likes better,
And folden faith to that fre, festned so harde
That you lausen ne list; and that I leve nowthe,
1785 And that ye telle me that now truly I pray you.
For alle the lufes upon live, laine not the sothe
            for gile."
        The knight said, "By Sain Jon,"
        And smethely con he smile,
1790   "In faith I welde right none,
        Ne none wil welde the while."

"That is a worde," quoth that wight, "that worst is of alle;
Bot I am swared for sothe, that sore me thinkes.
Kisse me now comly, and I shal cach hethen;
1795 I may bot mourne upon molde, as may that much loves."
Sikande ho sweghe doun and semly him kissed,
And sithen ho severes him fro, and says as ho stondes,
"Now, dere, at this departing do me this ese:
Give me sumwhat of thy gift, thy glove if hit were,
1800 That I may minne on the, mon, my mourning to lassen."

1803 *sellily:* very
1804 *reche:* offer
1805 *dawed:* would avail
     neked: little
1807 *garisoun:* keepsake
1808 *an erand:* on a mission
     erdes uncouthe: unknown
       regions
1809 *males:* cases
     menskful: valuable
1810 *mislikes:* displeases, sad-
      dens
1811 *mon:* must
1812 *pine:* grief
1814 *lufsum under line:* fair lady
     (literally, lovely one under
     linen)
1817 *raght:* offered
1818 *starande:* shining
     stondande aloft: standing
      out
1819 *blushande:* gleaming
1820 *Wit ye wel:* be assured

1821 *renayed:* refused
1822 *for good:* to keep
1823 *nurne:* offer
1826 *sory:* was grieved
     forsoke: refused
1827 *renay:* refuse
     to: too
1828 *highly holden:* deeply in-
      debted
1829 *gaines:* is of use
1830 *leke:* fastened
     umbe: about
1831 *knit:* knotted
     kirtel: tunic
1832 *Gered:* fashioned
     shaped: adorned
1833 *Noght bot:* only
     braiden: embroidered
     beten: set
1836 *garisoun:* treasure
1840 *businesse:* importunity
     baithe: consent

"Now iwis," quoth that wighe, "I wolde I had here
The levest thing for thy luf that I in londe welde,
For ye have deserved, for sothe, sellily oft
More rewarde by resoun then I reche might;
1805 Bot to dele you for drury, that dawed bot neked,
Hit is not your honour to have at this time
A glove for a garisoun of Gawaines giftes;
And I am here an erand in erdes uncouthe
And have no men with no males with menskful thinges;
1810 That mislikes me, lady, for luf at this time;
Uche tulk mon do as he is tan; tas to none ille
        ne pine."
        "Nay, hende of high honours,"
        Quoth that lufsum under line,
1815   "Thagh I had noght of youres,
        Yet shulde ye have of mine."

Ho raght him a rich ring of red gold werkes,
With a starande stone stondande aloft
That bere blushande bemes as the bright sunne;
1820 Wit ye wel, hit was worth wele ful huge.
Bot the renk hit renayed, and redily he said,
"I wil no giftes for good, my gay, at this time;
I have none you to nurne, ne noght wil I take."
Ho bede hit him ful busily, and he hir bode wernes,
1825 And swere swifte by his sothe that he hit sese nolde;
And ho sory that he forsoke, and said thereafter,
"If ye renay my ring, to rich for hit semes,
Ye wolde not so highly holden be to me,
I shal give you my girdel, that gaines you lasse."
1830 Ho laght a lace lightly that leke umbe hir sides,
Knit upon hir kirtel under the clere mantile;
Gered hit was with grene silk and with gold shaped,
Noght bot arounde braiden, beten with fingeres;
And that ho bede to the burn, and blithely besoght,
1835 Thagh hit unworthy were, that he hit take wolde.
And he nay that he nolde negh in no wise
Nauther gold ne garisoun, ere God him grace sende
To acheve to the chaunce that he had chosen there.
"And therfore, I pray you, displese you not,
1840 And lettes be your businesse, for I baithe hit you never
        to grant;

1842 *derely:* deeply
1843 *semblaunt:* kindly manner
1846 *forsake:* refuse
1849 *gorde:* girt
1852 *hemely:* neatly
 halched: fastened round
1853 *tohewe:* cut down, kill
1854 *for sleght upon erthe:* by
 any means
1856 *juel:* jewel
 jugged: adjudged, assigned
1857 *chek:* fate
 fech: receive
1858 *slipped:* escaped
 sleght: device
1859 *thulged:* was patient
 threpe: importunity
 tholed: allowed
1860 *bere:* pressed
 swithe: earnestly
1861 *granted:* consented
1862 *discover:* reveal
1863 *laine:* conceal
1864 *wit:* know
1866 *swithe:* greatly
1867 *thro:* earnestly
1868 *on thrinne sithe:* for the
 third time
1869 *toght:* courteous
1872 *geres:* clothes
1873 *riches him:* dresses
1874 *raght:* gave
1875 *holdely:* carefully
1876 *chefly:* quickly
1877 *prest:* priest
1879 *seye hethen:* go away
1880 *shrof:* confessed
1881 *minne:* smaller
1882 *on the segg calles:* begs the
 man (i.e. the priest) for

I am derely to you beholde
Because of your semblaunt
And ever in hot and colde
1845   To be your true servaunt."

"Now forsake ye this silk," said the burde then,
"For hit is simple in hitself?   And so hit wel semes.
Lo, so hit is littel, and lasse hit is worthy;
Bot whoso knew the costes that knit are therinne,
1850 He wolde hit praise at more pris, paraventure;
For what gome is gorde with this grene lace,
While he hit had hemely halched aboute,
There is no hathel under heven tohewe him that might,
For he might not be slain for sleght upon erthe."
1855 Then cast the knight, and hit come to his hert,
Hit were a juel for the jopardy that him jugged were
When he acheved to the chapel his chek for to fech;
Might he have slipped to be unslain, the sleght were noble.
Then he thulged with hir threpe and tholed hir to speke,
1860 And ho bere on him the belt and bede hit him swithe,
And he granted; and him gave with a good wille,
And besoght him, for hir sake, discover hit never,
Bot to lelly laine fro hir lorde; the leude him accordes
That never wighe shulde hit wit, iwis, bot thay twaine
1855   for noght;
He thonked hir oft ful swithe,
Ful thro with hert and thoght.
By that on thrinne sithe
Ho has kist the knight so toght.

1870 Then laches ho hir leve, and leves him there,
For more mirthe of that mon moght ho not gete.
When ho was gon, Sir Gawain geres him sone,
Rises and riches him in aray noble,
Lays up the luf-lace the lady him raght,
1875 Hid hit ful holdely, there he hit eft founde.
Sithen chefly to the chapel choses he the waye,
Privily aproched to a prest, and prayed him there
That he wolde lifte his lif and lern him better
How his saule shulde be saved when he shuld seye hethen.
1880 There he shrof him shirely and shewed his misdedes,
Of the more and the minne, and mercy beseches,
And of absolucioun he on the segg calles;

1883 *asoiled:* absolved
1884 *alle kinnes:* all kinds of
1889 *dainty:* courteous treatment
1892 *Sin:* since
1893 *lee:* comfortable place
1895 *forfaren:* killed
    folged: followed
1896 *sprent:* leapt
    spenny: spinney
    shrewe: villain
1897 *hasted:* pressed (in pursuit)
    swith: hard
1898 *richande:* making his way
1899 *res:* rush
1900 *wilde:* wild animals
1902 *shunt:* swerved
    arered: drawn back
1903 *rapes:* hastens
1905 *wroth:* fierce
1907 *Rased:* snatched
1909 *brothe:* fierce
1911 *rechatande:* blowing the
    recall (see note on l. 1446)
1915 *mute:* baying of hounds
1916 *rurd:* noise
1919 *fawne:* fondle
    frote: rub, stroke
1921 *helden:* went
1923 *Strakande:* sounding
    stor: mighty

And he asoiled him surely, and sette him so clene
As domesday shulde have bene dight on the morn.
1885 And sithen he mas him as mery among the fre ladies,
With comlich caroles and alle kinnes joy,
As never he did bot that day, to the derk night,
                    with blisse.
                Uche mon had dainty there
1890   Of him, and said, "Iwis,
                Thus mery he was never ere,
                Sin he com hider, ere this."

Now him lenge in that lee, there luf him betide!
Yet is the lord on the launde ledande his games;
1895 He has forfaren this fox that he folged long;
As he sprent over a spenny to spye the shrewe,
There as he herd the houndes that hasted him swithe,
Reynarde com richande thurgh a rugh greve,
And alle the rabel in a res right at his heles.
1900 The wighe was ware of the wilde, and warely abides,
And braides out the bright bronde, and at the best castes.
And he shunt for the sharp, and shulde have arered;
A rach rapes him to, right ere he might,
And right before the horse fete thay fel on him alle,
1905 And woried me this wily with a wroth noise.
The lord lightes bilive, and laches him sone,
Rased him ful radly out of the rach mouthes,
Holdes high over his hed, halowes faste,
And there bayen him mony brothe houndes.
1910 Huntes highed hem thider with hornes ful mony,
Ay rechatande aright til thay the renk seghen.
By that was comen his companie noble,
Alle that ever ber bugle blowed at ones,
And alle these other halowed that had no hornes;
1915 Hit was the meriest mute that ever men herde,
The rich rurd that there was raised for Reynarde saule
                    with lote.
                Hor houndes thay there rewarde,
                Her hedes thay fawne and frote,
1920   And sithen thay tan Reynarde
                And tirven of his cote.

And then thay helden to home, for hit was negh night,
Strakande ful stoutly in hor stor hornes.

1926 *withalle:* entirely
1927 *ladde:* had
1928 *bleaunt:* mantle of rich material
   bradde: reached
1929 *semed:* suited
1931 *Blande:* adorned
   blaunner: fur (ermine?)
1933 *gret:* greeted
1934 *fille:* fulfil
   nowthe: now
1935 *spedly:* with good results
1936 *acoles:* embraces
1937 *savourly:* with relish
   sadly: firmly
1938 *sele:* good fortune
1939 *chevisaunce:* obtaining
   chaffer: merchandise
   chepes: bargains
1940 *chepe:* price
   no charge: it does not matter
   chefly: quickly
1941 *pertly:* openly
   chepes: goods
   aghte: had
1944 *fende:* devil
1945 *pris:* precious
1946 *thright:* pressed on
   thro: heartily
   cosses: kisses
1949 *rode:* cross
1954 *bourdes:* jests
1956 *doted:* gone silly
1958 *seyen:* come
   moste: must
1961 *Foches:* takes
1962 *selly:* excellent
1964 *yef:* give
1965 *to-morn:* tomorrow morning

The lord is light at the last at his lef home

1925 Findes fire upon flet, the freke therbeside,
Sir Gawain the good, that glad was withalle,
Among the ladies for luf he ladde much joy;
He were a bleaunt of blue that bradde to the erthe,
His surcote semed him wel that soft was furred,

1930 And his hode of that ilke henged on his shulder,
Blande al of blaunner were both al aboute.
He metes me this good mon inmiddes the flore,
And al with gamen he him gret, and goodly he said,
"I shal fille upon first oure forwardes nowthe,

1935 That we spedly han spoken, there spared was no drink."
Then acoles he the knight and kisses him thrise,
As savourly and sadly as he hem sette couth.
"By Crist," quoth that other knight, "ye cach much sele
In chevisaunce of this chaffer, if ye had good chepes."

1940 "Ye, of the chepe no charge," quoth chefly that other,
"As is pertly payed the chepes that I aghte."
"Mary," quoth that other mon, "myn is behinde,
For I have hunted al this day, and noght have I geten
Bot this foule fox felle—the fende have the goodes!

1945 And that is ful pore for to pay for such pris thinges
As ye have thright me here thro, such thre cosses
so good."
"Innowe," quoth Sir Gawain,
"I thonk you, by the rode,"

1950 And how the fox was slain
He tolde him as thay stode.

With mirthe and minstralsie, with metes at hor wille,
Thay maden as mery as any men moghten,
With laghing of ladies, with lotes of bourdes—

1955 Gawain and the good mon so glad were thay both—
Bot if the douth had doted, other dronken bene other.
Both the mon and the meiny maden mony japes,
Til the sesoun was seyen that thay sever moste;
Burnes to hor bed behoved at the last.

1960 Then lowly his leve at the lord first
Foches this fre mon, and fair he him thonkes:
"Of such a selly sojourne as I have had here,
Your honour at this high fest, the high king you yelde!
I yef you me for one of youres, if yourself likes—

1965 For I mot nedes, as ye wot, meve to-morn—

1968 *dome:* judgement
wirdes: fate
1972 *coundue:* conduct
downes: hills
drech: trouble
1973 *frith:* wood
at the gainest: by the most
direct route
1976 *worship:* honourable treatment
weve: offer
1979 *til:* to
1980 *thrivande:* hearty
thrat: urged
1981 *yeply:* promptly
1982 *bekende:* commended
sikings: sighs
1983 *menskly:* courteously
1984 *made hem a thonke:* gave
them his thanks
1985 *sere:* individual, personal
pine: trouble
1986 *businesse:* solicitude
1987 *sory:* was grieved
sever: part
1992 *minne:* think of
1995 *soght:* was making for
2000 *wederes:* storms
2001 *kenely:* bitterly

And ye me take sum tulk to teche, as ye hight,
The gate to the grene chapel, as God wil me suffer
To dele on New Yeres day the dome of my wirdes."
"In good faith," quoth the good mon, "with a good wille
1970 Al that ever I you hight holde shal I redy."
There asignes he a servaunt to sett him in the way,
And coundue him by the downes, that he no drech had,
For to ferk thurgh the frith and fare at the gainest
                    by greve.
1975   The lord Gawain con thonk,
            Such worship he wolde him weve.
            Then at tho ladies wlonk
            The knight has tan his leve.

With care and with kissing he carpes hem til,
1980 And fele thrivande thonkes he thrat hom to have,
And thay yelden him again yeply that ilk;
Thay bekende him to Crist with ful colde sikinges.
Sithen fro the meiny he menskly departes;
Uche mon that he mette, he made hem a thonke
1985 For his service and his solace and his sere pine,
That thay with businesse had bene aboute him to serve;
And uche segg as sory to sever with him there
As thay had woned worthily with that wlonk ever.
Then with leudes and light he was ladde to his chamber
1990 And blithely broght to his bed to be at his rest.
If he ne slepe soundily, say ne dar I,
For he had much on the morn to minne, if he wolde,
                    in thoght.
            Let him lie there stille,
1995   He has nere that he soght;
            And ye wil a while be stille
            I shal telle you how thay wroght.

———————

IV

Now neghes the New Yere, and the night passes,
The day drives to the derk, as Drightin biddes;
2000 Bot wilde wederes of the worlde wakened theroute,
Cloudes casten kenely the colde to the erthe,

2002 *nye:* bitterness
    tene: torment
2003 *snitered:* came shivering down
    snart: bitterly
    snaiped: nipped cruelly
    wilde: wild creatures
2004 *werbelande:* blowing shrilly
    wapped: rushed
2007 *loukes:* shuts
    liddes: eyelids
2008 *steven:* appointed day
2009 *Deliverly:* quickly
    dressed up: got up
    sprenged: broke
2011 *cofly:* promptly
    swared: answered
2012 *bruny:* shirt of mail
2015 *were:* ward off
2016 *harnais:* armour
    holdely: carefully
2017 *paunce:* armour covering abdomen
    piked: polished

2018 *rokked:* burnished
    roust: rust
2023 *into Grece:* from here to Greece
2025 *warp:* put
2026 *conisaunce:* badge
2027 *Ennurned:* set as ornament
    vertuous: precious
2028 *beten:* set
    semes: ornamental stitching about seams
2032 *balgh:* smooth
2033 *dressed:* arranged
2034 *Swithe:* quickly
    swethled: wrapped
    umbe: about
    swange: waist
2039 *glent:* glinted
2041 *bale:* death
    debate: resistance
    were: defend

With nye innowe of the northe, the naked to tene;
The snaw snitered ful snart, that snaiped the wilde;
The werbelande winde wapped fro the high,
2005 And drof uche dale ful of driftes ful gret.
The leude listened ful wel that lay in his bed,
Thagh he loukes his liddes, ful littel he slepes;
By uche cok that crewe he knew wel the steven.
Deliverly he dressed up, ere the day sprenged,
2010 For there was light of a laumpe that lemed in his chamber;
He called to his chamberlain, that cofly him swared,
And bede him bring his bruny and his blonk sadel;
That other ferkes him up and feches him his wedes,
And graithes me Sir Gawain upon a gret wise.
2015 First he clad him in his clothes the colde for to were,
And sithen his other harnais, that holdely was keped,
Both his paunce and his plates, piked ful clene,
The ringes rokked of the roust of his rich bruny;
And al was fresh as upon first, and he was fain then
2020   to thonk;
          He had upon uche pece,
          Wiped ful wel and wlonk;
          The gayest into Grece,
          The burn bede bring his blonk.

2025 While the wlonkest wedes he warp on himselven,
His cote with the conisaunce of the clere werkes
Ennurned upon velvet, vertuous stones
Aboute beten and bounden, enbrawded semes,
And ferly furred withinne with fair pelures,
2030 Yet laft he not the lace, the ladies gift;
That forgat not Gawain for good of himselven.
By he had belted the bronde upon his balgh haunches,
Then dressed he his drury double him aboute,
Swithe swethled umbe his swange swetely that knight
2035 The girdel of the grene silk, that gay wel besemed,
Upon that royal red clothe that rich was to shewe.
Bot wered not this ilk wighe for wele this girdel,
For pride of the pendauntes, thagh polised thay were,
And thagh the gliterande gold glent upon endes,
2040 Bot for to saven himself, when suffer him behoved,
To bide bale withoute debate of bronde him to were
                   other knif.

2043 *boun:* ready, dressed
2044 *Winnes:* comes
2046 *rive:* abundantly
2048 *savourly:* to his liking
　　in a siker wise: securely
2049 *prik:* spur, gallop
　　for point: he was in such
　　　good condition
2050 *winnes:* goes
　　wites: looks
　　lere: flesh OR face
2051 *sweres:* swears
2052 *mote:* castle
　　mensk: courtesy
2054 *on live:* all her life
2055 *cherishen:* receive kindly
2059 *rech:* offer
2062 *Girdes to:* applies the spurs
　　　to
2067 *kenne:* commend
2068 *gave hit ay good chaunce:*
　　　wished it good fortune
　　　for ever
2071 *bredes:* boards
2075 *tene:* perilous
2076 *race:* onslaught
　　resaive: receive
2077 *boghes:* boughs
2078 *clomben:* climbed
　　clenges: clings
2079 *halt:* lifted
2080 *muged:* drizzled, was damp
　　mor: moor
　　malt: melted
2081 *mist-hakel:* cloak of mist
2082 *brokes:* brooks
　　breke: foamed
2083 *shaterande:* dashing and
　　　breaking

By that the bold mon boun
Winnes theroute bilive,
2045   Alle the meiny of renoun
He thonkes oft ful rive.

Then was Gringolet graithe, that gret was and huge,
And had bene sojourned savourly and in a siker wise;
Him list prik for point, that proude horse then.
2050 The wighe winnes him to and wites on his lere,
And said soberly himself and by his sothe sweres:
"Here is a meiny in this mote that on mensk thenkes.
The mon hem mainteines, joy mot he have;
The leve lady on live, luf hir betide;
2055 If thay for charity cherishen a gest,
And holden honour in her hand, the hathel hem yelde
That holdes the heven upon high, and also you alle!
And if I might lif upon londe lede any while,
I shuld rech you sum rewarde redily, if I might."
2060 Then steppes he into stirop and strides aloft;
His shalk shewed him his shelde, on shulder he hit laght,
Girdes to Gringolet with his gilt heles,
And he startes on the stone, stod he no lenger
              to praunce.
2065   His hathel on horse was then,
That bere his spere and lance.
"This castel to Crist I kenne;"
He gave hit ay good chaunce.

The brige was braide doun, and the brode gates
2070 Unbarred and born open upon both half.
The burn blessed him bilive, and the bredes passed,
Praises the porter before the prince kneled,
Gave him God and good day, that Gawain he save,
And went on his way with his wighe one,
2075 That shulde teche him to turne to that tene place
There the ruful race he shulde resaive.
Thay bowen by bonkes there boghes are bare,
Thay clomben by cliffes there clenges the colde;
The heven was up-halt, bot ugly therunder,
2080 Mist muged on the mor, malt on the mountes,
Uche hille had a hatte, a mist-hakel huge.
Brokes boiled and breke by bonkes aboute,
Shire shaterance on shores, there thay doun showved.

2084 *Wela:* very
wille: wandering, perplexing
2092 *nare ye not:* you are not
note: notorious
2093 *spied:* looked for
spured: asked
2095 *upon live:* alive, on earth
2096 *worthed:* would fare
2097 *prese:* hasten
2100 *upon middelerde:* on earth
2102 *Hestor:* Hector (of Troy)
2103 *cheves that chaunce:* brings
it to pass
2105 *dinges:* strikes
2106 *methles:* violent, without
restraint
2107 *chorle:* man of low birth
2108 *masseprest:* priest
2109 *queme:* pleasant
quelle: kill
quik: alive
2111 *Com ye:* if you go
may the knight rede: if the
knight has his way
2114 *yore:* a long time
2115 *baret:* strife, trouble
bende: brought about
2116 *Again:* against
2120 *kith:* land
spede: prosper, help
2121 *hete:* promise
2122 *swere:* swear
halghes: saints
2123 *Halidam:* all that is holy
2124 *you laine:* keep your secret

Wela wille was the way there thay by wod shulden,
2085 Til hit was sone sesoun that the sunne rises
                    that tide.
            Thay were on a hille ful high,
            The white snaw lay beside;
            The burn that rode him by
2090   Bede his maister abide.

"For I have wonnen you hider, wighe, at this time,
And now nare ye not fer fro that note place
That ye han spied and spured so specially after;
Bot I shal say you for sothe, sithen I you knowe,
2095 And ye are a leude upon live that I wel love,
Wolde ye worche by my wit, ye worthed the better.
The place that ye prese to ful perilous is holden;
There wones a wighe in that waste, the worst upon erthe,
For he is stif and sturn, and to strike loves,
2100 And more is he then any mon upon middelerde,
And his body bigger then the best foure
That are in Arthures hous, Hestor, other other.
He cheves that chaunce at the chapel grene,
There passes none by that place so proude in his armes
2105 That he ne dinges him to dethe with dint of his hand;
For he is a mon methles, and mercy none uses,
For be hit chorle other chaplain that by the chapel rides,
Monk other masseprest, other any mon elles,
Him think as queme him to quelle as quik go himselven.
2110 Forthy I say the, as sothe as ye in sadel sitte,
Com ye there, ye be killed, may the knight rede,
Trawe ye me that truly, thagh ye had twenty lives
                    to spende.
            He has woned here ful yore,
2115   On bent much baret bende,
            Again his dintes sore
            Ye may not you defende.

"Forthy, good Sir Gawain, let the gome one,
And gos away sum other gate, upon Goddes half!
2120 Cayres by sum other kith, there Crist mot you speed,
And I shal high me home again, and hete you firre
That I shal swere by God and alle his good halghes,
As help me God and the halidam, and othes innowe,
That I shal lelly you laine, and lance never tale

2125 *fondet:* attempted
2126 *gruching:* reluctantly
2127 *Wel worth the:* may you have good fortune
2128 *me laine:* keep my secret
leve: believe
2129 *holde:* loyally
2130 *Founded:* hastened
2132 *for chaunce that may falle:* whatever may happen
2134 *Worthe hit wele other wo:* whether good or ill comes of it
the wirde: fate
2136 *knape:* fellow
2137 *stightel:* deal with
2138 *shape:* contrive
2140 *spelles:* sayest
2141 *nye:* harm
nime to: take upon
2142 *lese:* lose
lette: hinder
kepe: care
2144 *rake:* path
2146 *lift:* left
2147 *slade:* valley
2148 *borelich:* strong
2151 *bere the felaghship:* keep you company
frith: wood
2157 *grete:* weep
2158 *bain:* obedient
2159 *tone:* committed
2160 *girdes:* applies spurs
gederes the rake: takes the path
2161 *shawe:* small wood
2163 *waited:* looked
2164 *resette:* shelter
2165 *brent:* steep

2125 That ever ye fondet to fle for freke that I wist."
"Grant merci," quoth Gawain, and gruching he said:
"Wel worth the, wighe, that woldes my good,
And that lelly me laine I leve wel thou woldes.
Bot helde thou hit never so holde, and I here passed,
2130 Founded for ferde for to fle, in forme that thou telles,
I were a knight cowarde, I might not be excused.
Bot I wil to the chapel, for chaunce that may falle,
And talk with that ilk tulk the tale that me liste,
Worthe hit wele other wo, as the wirde likes
2135   hit have.
            Thagh he be a sturn knape
            To stightel, and stad with stave,
            Ful wel con Drightin shape
            His servauntes for to save."

2140 "Mary!" quoth that other mon, "now thou so much spelles,
That thou wilt thyn owen nye nime to thyselven,
And the list lese thy lif, the lette I ne kepe.
Have here thy helme on thy hed, thy spere in thy hand,
And ride me doun this ilk rake by yon rokke side,
2145 Til thou be broght to the bothem of the breme valay;
Then loke a littel on the launde, on thy lift hand,
And thou shal se in that slade the self chapel,
And the borelich burn on bent that hit kepes.
Now fares wel, on Goddes half, Gawain the noble!
2150 For alle the gold upon grounde I nolde go with the,
Ne bere the felaghship thurgh this frith one fote firre."
By that the wighe in the wod wendes his bridel,
Hit the horse with the heles as hard as he might,
Lepes him over the launde, and leves the knight there
2155   alone.
            "By Goddes self," quoth Gawain,
            "I wil nauther grete ne grone;
            To Goddes wille I am ful bain,
            And to him I have me tone."

2160 Then girdes he to Gringolet, and gederes the rake,
Showves in by a shore at a shawe side,
Rides thurgh the rugh bonk right to the dale;
And then he waited him aboute, and wilde hit him thoght,
And seghe no signe of resette besides nowhere,
2165 Bot high bonkes and brent upon both half,

2166 *knokled:* rugged
knarres: gnarled rocks
knorned: gnarled
2167 *skewes:* clouds
of the scowtes: by the jutting rocks
skained: grazed
2168 *hoved:* stopped
2170 *selly:* strange
2171 *lawe:* mound
2172 *balgh:* smooth
berg: mound
2173 *fors:* waterfall
flode: stream
2174 *borne:* stream
blubred: bubbled
2175 *caches:* urges on
caple: horse
lawe: mound
2176 *linde:* lime-tree
taches: fastens
2177 *raine:* rein
rich: noble (horse)
2181 *gresse:* grass
glodes: patches
2182 *holgh:* hollow
inwith: within
2183-84 *deme hit with spelle:* make it out, say (what it was)

2186 *Whether this be:* can this be
2188 *dele:* devil
2189 *wisty:* desolate
2190 *oritore:* oratory, chapel
2191 *wruxled:* wrapped
2193 *fele:* feel
fende: devil
2194 *stoken:* imposed on
steven: appointment
strye: destroy
2195 *chek:* bad luck
2198 *romes:* wanders
2202 *grindelstone:* grindstone
sythe: scythe
2203 *wharred:* whirred
mulne: mill
2204 *rawthe:* grievous
here: hear
2205 *gere:* business (i.e. the noise of sharpening a weapon)
2206 *Is riched at the reverence me, renk, to mete:* is intended for the honour of meeting me (i.e. has been deliberately arranged to give me an impressive reception)
2207 *by rote:* on (my) way

And rugh knokled knarres with knorned stones;
The skewes of the scowtes skained him thoght.
Then he hoved, and withhelde his horse at that tide,
And oft chaunged his chere the chapel to seche.
2170 He segh none such in no side, and selly him thoght
Sone, a littel on a launde, a lawe as hit were;
A balgh bergh by a bonk the brimme beside,
By a fors of a flode that ferked there;
The borne blubred therinne as hit boiled had.
2175 The knight caches his caple, and com to the lawe,
Lightes doun luflily, and at a linde taches
The raine and his rich with a rugh braunch.
Then he bowes to the bergh, aboute hit he walkes,
Debatande with himself what hit be might.
2180 Hit had a hole on the ende and on aither side,
And overgrowen with gresse in glodes aywhere,
And al was holgh inwith, nobot an olde cave,
Or a crevisse of an olde cragge, he couth hit not deme
                    with spelle.
2185   "We! Lord," quoth the gentile knight,
             "Whether this be the grene chapel?
             Here might aboute midnight
             The dele his matines telle!

"Now, iwis," quoth Wawain, "wisty is here;
2190 This oritore is ugly, with erbes overgrowen;
Wel besemes the wighe wruxled in grene
Dele here his devocioun on the develes wise.
Now I fele hit is the fende, in my five wittes,
That has stoken me this steven to strye me here.
2195 This is a chapel of meschaunce, that chek hit betide!
Hit is the corsedest kirk that ever I com inne!"
With high helme on his hed, his lance in his hand,
He romes up to the rokke of tho rugh wones.
Then herde he of that high hille, in a hard roche
2200 Beyonde the broke, in a bonk, a wonder breme noise.
Quat! hit clatered in the cliff, as hit cleve shulde,
As one upon a grindelstone had grounden a sythe.
What! hit wharred and whette, as water at a mulne;
What! hit rushed and ronge, rawthe to here.
2205 Then, "By God," quoth Gawain, "that gere, as I trowe,
Is riched at the reverence me, renk, to mete
                    by rote.

2208 *we lo:* ah well
2209 *mote:* jot
2211 *Drede dos me no lote:* no
noise can frighten me
2213 *stightles:* is master
steven: appointment
2215 *winne:* come
2216 *nedes:* business
spede: get done
2219 *rurd:* noise
rapely: hastily
a throwe: for a time
2220 *awharf:* turned away
2221 *keveres:* makes his way
2222 *wro:* nook
2223 *Denes:* Danish
dight: set, made
2224 *borelich:* massive
halme: handle
2225 *Filed:* sharpened
filor: whetstone
2227 *gered:* clothed and equip-
ped
2228 *lyre:* face
2229 *foundes:* hastens
2230 *stele:* handle
2231 *wan to:* reached
2232 *hipped:* hopped, jumped
2233 *brothe:* fierce
2236 *lut:* bowed before
2238 *steven:* appointment
2239 *loke:* guard
2241 *travail:* arduous journey
2244 *yepely:* promptly
2246 *ridde:* separate
rele: sway, stagger in
combat
2248 *debate:* resistance

Let God worche, we lo!
Hit helpes me not a mote.
2210 My lif thagh I forgo,
Drede dos me no lote."

Then the knight con calle ful high:
"Who stightles in this stedde me steven to holde?
For now is good Gawain goande right here.
2215 If any wighe oght wil, winne hider fast,
Other now other never, his nedes to spede."
"Abide," quoth one on the bonk aboven over his hed,
"And thou shal have al in haste that I the hight ones."
Yet he rushed on that rurd rapely a throwe,
2220 And with whetting awharf, ere he wolde light;
And sithen he keveres by a cragge, and comes of a hoie,
Whirlande out of a wro with a felle weppen,
A Denes axe newe dight, the dint with to yelde,
With a borelich bit bende by the halme,
2225 Filed in a filor, foure fote large—
Hit was no lasse by that lace that lemed ful bright—
And the gome in the grene gered as first,
Both the lyre and the legges, lokkes and berde;
Save that fair on his fote he foundes on the erthe,
2230 Sette the stele to the stone, and stalked beside.
When he wan to the water, there he wade nolde,
He hipped over on his axe, and orpedly strides,
Bremely brothe on a bent that brode was aboute,
on snaw.
2235 Sir Gawain the knight con mete,
He ne lut him nothing lowe;
That other said, "Now, sir swete,
Of steven mon may the trowe."

"Gawain," quoth that grene gome, "God the mot loke!
2240 Iwis thou art welcom, wighe, to my place,
And thou has timed thy travail as true mon shulde,
And thou knowes the convenauntes cast us betwene:
At this time twelmonith thou toke that the falled,
And I shulde at this New Yere yepely the quite.
2245 And we are in this valay veraily oure one;
Here are no renkes us to ridde, rele as us likes.
Have thy helme of thy hed, and have here thy pay.
Busk no more debate then I the bede then

119

2249 *wap:* blow
2250 *me gost lante:* gave me a soul
2251 *gruch:* bear a grudge
     no grue: not at all
     greme: hurt
2252 *stightel the upon:* restrict yourself to
2253 *warp:* offer
     werning: resistance
2254 *nowhare:* not at all
2255 *lutte:* bowed
2257 *dutte:* feared
2258 *dare:* tremble, cower
2259 *swithe:* quickly
2260 *tole:* weapon
2261 *bur:* strength
     on loft: aloft
2262 *munt:* swung, took aim
     maghtily: forcibly
     marre: destroy
2263 *drighe:* hard, powerfully
     atled: intended, prepared
2265 *giserne:* battle-axe
     glifte: glanced
2266 *glidande:* gliding
     glode: ground
     shende: destroy

2267 *irne:* iron
2268 *shunt:* sudden sideways movement
     shene: shining (blade)
2269 *repreved:* rebuked
2271 *arghed:* was afraid
     here: company of warriors
2272 *for ferde:* in fear
     fele: feel
2274 *fiked:* flinched
     flagh: dodged
     thou mintest: you took aim
2275 *cast no cavelacioun:* raised no quibble
2276 *hed flagh:* head flew
     flagh I: I dodged
2277 *thou arghes:* you are terrified
2278 *me burde:* I ought to be
2280 *shunt:* flinched
2284 *bring me to the point:* come to the point with me
2288 *heves:* lifts
2289 *waites:* looks
     wrothely: fiercely
     wode: mad

When thou wipped of my hed at a wap one."
2250 "Nay, by God," quoth Gawain, "that me gost lante,
I shal gruch the no grue for greme that falles.
Bot stightel the upon one stroke, and I shal stonde stille
And warp the no werning to worch as the likes,
                    nowhare."
2255   He lened with the nek, and lutte,
                   And shewed that shire al bare,
                   And lette as he noght dutte;
                   For drede he wolde not dare.

Then the gome in the grene graithed him swithe,
2260 Gederes up his grimme tole Gawain to smite;
With alle the bur in his body he ber hit on loft,
Munt as maghtily as marre him he wolde;
Had hit driven adoun as drighe as he atled,
There had bene ded of his dint that doghty was ever.
2265 Bot Gawain on that giserne glifte him beside
As hit com glidande adoun on glode him to shende,
And shranke a littel with the shulderes for the sharp irne.
That other shalk with a shunt the shene witholdes;
And then repreved he the prince with many proude wordes:
2270 "Thou art not Gawain," quoth the gome, "that is so good holden,
That never arghed for no here by hille ne by vale,
And now thou fles for ferde ere thou fele harmes!
Such cowardise of that knight couth I never here.
Nauther fiked I ne flagh, freke, when thou mintest,
2275 Ne cast no cavelacioun in kinges hous Arthur.
My hed flagh to my fote, and yet flagh I never;
And thou, ere any harme hent, arghes in hert;
Wherfore the better burn me burde be called
                    therfore."
2280   Quoth Gawain, "I shunt ones,
                   And so wil I no more;
                   Bot thagh my hed falle on the stones
                   I con not hit restore.

"Bot busk, burn, by thy faith, and bring me to the point;
2285 Dele to me my destiny, and do hit out of hand,
For I shal stonde the a stroke, and start no more
Til thyn axe have me hitte, have here my trauthe."
"Have at the then!" quoth that other, and heves hit aloft,
And waites as wrothely as he wode were.

2290 *mintes:* takes aim
maghtily: forcibly
rives: cuts
2292 *glent:* flinched
membre: limb
2293 *stubbe:* tree-stump
2294 *ratheled:* entwined
rochy: rocky
2297 *raght:* gave
2298 *kanel:* neck, wind-pipe
cast: blow, stroke
kever: survive
2299 *grindelly:* wrathfully
greme: anger
2300 *thro:* fierce
to: too
2301 *hope:* think
arghe: is frightened
2303 *on lite:* in delay
lette: hinder
2305 *strithe:* stance
2306 *frounses:* puckers
2307 *him mislike:* it displeased
him (Gawain)

2308 *rescowe:* rescue
2309 *lome:* weapon
2311 *homered:* hammered
2312 *snirt:* cut slightly
2313 *shrank:* penetrated
grece: fat
2314 *shene:* bright
2315 *blenk:* glisten
2316 *sprit:* sprang
spenne-fote: with a kick
2320 *sin that:* since
2322 *Blinne:* cease
bur: violence
2323 *strif:* resistance
2324 *thou reches:* you offer
2325 *yederly:* promptly
therto ye trist: be sure of
that
2326 *foo:* fiercely
2328 *shop:* laid down
2329 *Fermed:* confirmed
2330 *hoo:* stop (whoa!)

2290 He mintes at him maghtily, bot not the mon rives,
Withhelde heterly his hand, ere hit hurt might.
Gawain graithely hit bides, and glent with no membre,
Bot stode stille as the stone, other a stubbe other
That ratheled is in rochy grounde with rotes a hundreth.
2295 Then merily eft con he mele, the mon in the grene:
"So now thou has thy hert hole; hitte me behoves.
Holde the now the high hode that Arthur the raght,
And kepe thy kanel at this cast, if hit kever may."
Gawain ful grindelly with greme then said:
2300 "Why, thresh on, thou thro mon; thou thretes to long.
I hope that thy hert arghe with thyn owen selven."
"For sothe," quoth that other freke, "so felly thou spekes,
I wil no lenger on lite lette thyn erand
                    right now."
2305   Then tas he him strithe to strike,
             And frounses both lippe and browe;
             No mervail thagh him mislike
             That hoped of no rescowe.

He liftes lightly his lome, and lette hit doun fair
2310 With the barbe of the bit by the bare nek;
Thagh he homered heterly, hurt him no more,
Bot snirt him on that one side, that severed the hide.
The sharp shrank to the flesh thurgh the shire grece,
That the shene blod over his shulderes shot to the erthe.
2315 And when the burn segh the blod blenk on the snaw,
He sprit forth spenne-fote more then a spere lenthe,
Hent heterly his helme, and on his hed cast,
Shot with his shulderes his fair shelde under,
Braides out a bright sworde, and bremely he spekes—
2320 Never sin that he was burn born of his moder
Was he never in this worlde wighe half so blithe—
"Blinne, burn, of thy bur; bede me no mo!
I have a stroke in this stedde withoute strif hent,
And if thou reches me any mo, I redily shal quite
2325 And yelde yederly again, and therto ye trist,
                    and foo.
             Bot one stroke here me falles;
             The covenaunt shop right so
             Shapen in Arthures halles.
2330   And therfore, hende, now hoo!"

123

2331 *heldet:* turned
2335 *aghles:* unafraid
2336 *much steven:* great voice
2337 *ringande rurd:* ringing noise
2338 *grindel:* fierce
2339-240 *No mon here unmanerly
the misboden habbes, ne
kidde:* Nobody here has
illtreated you (*misboden*),
nor shown you discourt-
esy (*kidde the unmanerly*)
2340 *shaped:* arranged
2343 *deliver:* nimble
paraunter: perhaps
2344 *wrotheloker:* more harshly
waret: dealt
anger: harm
2345 *mansed:* threatened
mint: feint
2346 *rove:* cut
rof: wound
2347 *fest:* agreed upon
2348 *tristily:* faithfully
trauthe: agreement
2350 *mint:* feint

2351 *cosses:* kisses
raghtes: gave
2352 *mintes:* feints
2353 *bout scathe:* without harm
2354 *True mon true restore:* let
a true man truly repay
2355 *thar:* need
wathe: danger
2357 *ta:* take
2359 *weved:* gave
2360 *cosses:* kisses
costes: qualities
2361 *wowing of:* wooing by
2362 *sende:* sent
assay: test
2364 *pese:* pea
2366 *lakked:* were at fault
leauty: loyalty
wonted: lacked
2367 *wilide werke:* intrigue
wowing: love-making
2370 *agreved:* weighed down
greme: mortification
gryed: cried in anguish
2371 *blende:* streamed together

The hathel heldet him fro, and on his axe rested,
Sette the shaft upon shore, and to the sharp lened,
And loked to the leude that on the launde yede,
How that doghty, dredles, derfly there stondes
2335 Armed, ful aghles; in hert hit him likes.
Then he meles merily with a much steven,
And with a ringande rurd he to the renk said,
"Bold burn, on this bent be not so grindel.
No mon here unmanerly the misboden habbes,
2340 Ne kidde, bot as covenaunt at kinges court shaped.
I hight the a stroke and thou hit has: holde the wel payed.
I relece the of the remnaunt of rights alle other.
If I deliver had bene, a buffet paraunter
I couth wrotheloker have waret, to the have wroght anger.
2345 First I mansed the merily with a mint one,
And rove the with no rof sore, with right I the profered
For the forward that we fest in the first night,
And thou tristily the trauthe and truly me holdes,
Al the gaine thou me gave, as good mon shulde.
2350 That other mint for the morn, mon, I the profered,
Thou kissedes my clere wif—the cosses me raghtes.
For both two here I the bede bot two bare mintes
bout scathe.
True mon true restore,
2355 Then thar mon drede no wathe.
At the thrid thou failed thore,
And therfore that tappe ta the.

"For hit is my wede that thou weres, that ilke woven girdel;
Myn owen wif hit the weved, I wot wel for sothe.
2360 Now know I wel thy cosses, and thy costes als,
And the wowing of my wif; I wroght hit myselven.
I sende hir to assay the, and sothly me thinkes
One the fautlest freke that ever on fote yede;
As perle by the white pese is of pris more,
2365 So is Gawain, in good faith, by other gay knightes.
Bot here you lakked a littel, sir, and leauty you wonted;
Bot that was for no wilide werke, ne wowing nauther,
Bot for ye lufed your lif; the lasse I you blame."
That other stif mon in study stod a gret while,
2370 So agreved for greme he gryed withinne;
Alle the blod of his brest blende in his face,
That al he shrank for shame that the shalk talked.

125

2373 *forme:* first
2375 *you:* you, i.e. cowardice and covetousness
disstryes: destroys
2376 *cast:* trick (i.e. the girdle)
lauses: unties
2377 *brothely:* fiercely
2378 *falssing:* false thing
foule mot hit falle: may evil befall it
2380 *kinde:* nature
2381 *largesse:* generosity
leauty: loyalty
longes to: befits
2382 *ferde:* afraid
2383 *sorewe:* sorrow
2385 *beknowe:* confess
2386 *fare:* conduct
2387 *overtake your wille:* understand what you wish me to do
2390 *hardily:* certainly
2391 *beknowen:* cleared by confession
misses: faults
2392 *apert:* evident
egge: edge, weapon
2393 *polised:* cleansed
plight: offence
2394 *forfeted:* transgressed
2397 *threpe:* contest
2401 *shin:* shall
2402 *bene:* pleasantly
2403 *lathed:* invited
fast: pressingly
2404 *wene:* think
2407 *sadly:* long enough
2410 *yare:* fully
yarkes: ordains
menskes: honour
2411 *comaundes:* commends
fere: wife
2413 *cast:* trick

The forme word upon folde that the freke meled:
"Corsed worth cowardise and covetise both!
2375 In you is vilany and vise that vertue disstryes."
Then he caght to the knot, and the cast lauses,
Braide brothely the belt to the burn selven:
"Lo, there the falssing, foule mot hit falle!
For care of thy knokke cowardise me taght
2380 To accorde me with covetise, my kinde to forsake,
That is largesse and leauty that longes to knightes.
Now I am fauty and false, and ferde have bene ever
Of trecherie and untrauthe; both betide sorewe
and care!
2385   I beknowe you, knight, here stille,
Al fauty is my fare.
Letes me overtake your wille,
And eft I shal be ware."

Then loghe that other leude and luflily said,
2390 "I holde hit hardily hole, the harme that I had.
Thou art confessed so clene, beknowen of thy misses,
And has the penaunce apert of the point of myn egge,
I holde the polised of that plight, and pured as clene
As thou hades never forfeted sithen thou was first born;
2395 And I give the, sir, the girdel that is gold-hemmed,
For hit is grene as my goune; Sir Gawain, ye maye
Thenk upon this ilke threpe, there thou forth thringes
Among princes of pris, and this a pure token
Of the chaunce at the grene chapel cf chevalrous knightes.
2400 And ye shal in this New Yere again to my wones,
And we shin revel the remnaunt of this rich fest
ful bene."
There lathed him fast the lord
And said, "With my wif, I wene,
2405   We shal you wel accorde,
That was your enmy kene."

"Nay, for sothe," quoth the segg, and sesed his helme,
And has hit of hendely, and the hathel thonkes,
"I have sojourned sadly; sele you betide,
2410 And he yelde hit you yare that yarkes al menskes!
And comaundes me to that cortais, your comlich fere,
Both that one and that other, myn honoured ladies,
That thus hor knight with hor cast han quaintly begiled.

127

2414 *ferly:* wonder
fole: fool
madde: acts madly
2415 *sorewe:* sorrow
2416 *in erde:* in fact
2417 *fele sere:* many and various
eftsones: again (for another example)
2418 *Dalida:* Delilah
wirde: fate
Davith: David
2419 *blended:* made blind
Barsabe: Bathsheba
bale: woe
tholed: endured
2420 *wrathed:* brought to disaster
winne: gain
2421 *leve:* believe
2422 *forne:* of old
that folged alle the sele: to all of whom prosperity came
2423 *Exellently of:* pre-eminently among
under hevenriche: on earth
2424 *mused:* were bemused (with love)

2425 *bewiled:* beguiled
2428 *me burde:* I ought to
2429 *foryelde:* reward
2430 *winne:* excellent
2431 *saint:* girdle
side: large
2433 *surfet:* transgression
2434 *remorde:* remember with remorse
2435 *faintise:* frailty
crabbed: perverse
2436 *entise:* attract
teches: stains
2437 *prik:* spur
2438 *The loke to:* a glance at
lethe: make humble
2440 *Sin:* since
lent: stayed
2443 *nurne:* call
2445 *hat:* am called
2446 *Morgne la Faye:* Morgane the Fairy
2447 *quaintise of clergie:* skill in magical learning
2448 *maistries:* arts
2449 *sumtime:* formerly
2450 *conable:* excellent
clerk: wizard
2454 *hawtesse:* pride

Bot hit is no ferly thagh a fole madde
2415 And thurgh wiles of wimmen be wonnen to sorewe,
For so was Adam in erde with one begiled,
And Salamon with fele sere, and Samson eftsones
Dalida dalt him his wirde, and Davith therafter
Was blended with Barsabe, that much bale tholed.
2420 Now these were wrathed with her wiles, hit were a winne huge
To luf hom wel and leve hem not, a leude that couthe.
For these were forne the freest, that folged alle the sele
Exellently of alle these other, under hevenriche
            that mused;
2425   And alle thay were bewiled
            With wimmen that thay used.
            Thagh I be now begiled,
            Me think me burde be excused.

"Bot your girdel," quoth Gawain, "God you foryelde!
2430 That wil I welde with good wille; not for the winne gold,
Ne the saint, ne the silk, ne the side pendauntes,
For wele ne for worship, ne for the wlonk werkes,
Bot in signe of my surfet I shal se hit oft,
When I ride in renoun, remorde to myselven
2435 The faut and the faintise of the flesh crabbed,
How tender hit is to entise teches of filthe;
And thus, when pride shal me prik for prowes of armes,
The loke to this luf-lace shal lethe my hert.
Bot one I wolde you pray, displeses you never:
2440 Sin ye be lord of the yonde londe there I have lent inne
With you with worship—the wighe hit you yelde
That upholdes the heven and on high sittes—
How nurne ye your right name?   And then no more."
"That shal I telle the truly," quoth that other then,
2445 "Bercilak de Hautdesert I hat in this londe.
Thurgh might of Morgne la Faye, that in my hous lenges,
And quaintise of clergie, by craftes wel lerned;
The maistries of Merlin, mony ho has taken;
For ho has dalt drury ful dere sumtime
2450 With that conable clerk, that knowes alle your knightes
            at hame;
            Morgne the goddes
            Therfore hit is hir name:
            Weldes none so high hawtesse
2455   That ho ne con make ful tame.

129

2456 *wained:* sent
winne: delightful
2457 *assay:* test
surquidry: pride
2459 *Ho wained me this wonder:*
she sent this wonder (*me*
is ethic dative)
reve: take away
2460 *Guenore:* Guenever
gart: caused
dighe: die
2461 *glopning:* dismay, terror
2465 *Tintagelle:* Tintagel (in
Cornwall)
Uter: Uther Pendragon
2466 *athel:* noble
nowthe: now
2467 *ethe:* entreat
2469 *wol the as wel:* wish you
as well
2471 *nikked him nay:* said "No"
to him
2472 *acolen:* embrace
kennen: commend

2475 *bene:* pleasing
2477 *enker:* bright
2481 *herbered:* lodged
al theroute: without any
shelter
2482 *in vale:* on the way
venquist: won ' victories
2483 *tight:* intend
2485 *blikkande:* gleaming
2486 *Abelef:* aslant
2487 *Loken:* fastened
lift: left
2488 *In tokening:* as a sign that
tan: caught
tech: stain
2489 *al in sounde:* in safety
2491 *gain:* a good thing
2493 *soght:* came
2494 *fare:* fortune
ferlily: , wondrously
2495 *Beknowes:* admits
costes of care: hardships

Ho wained me upon this wise to your winne halle
For to assay the surquidry, if hit sothe were
That rennes of the gret renoun of the Rounde Table;
Ho wained me this wonder your wittes to reve,
2460 For to have greved Guenore and gart hir to dighe
With glopning of that ilke gome that gostlich speked
With his hed in his hand before the high table.
That is ho that is at home, the auncian lady;
Ho is even thyn aunt, Arthures half-sister,
2465 The duches doghter of Tintagelle, that dere Uter after
Had Arthur upon, that athel is nowthe.
Therfore I ethe the, hathel, to com to thyn aunt;
Make mery in my hous; my meiny the loves,
And I wol the as wel, wighe, by my faith,
2470 As any gome under God for thy gret trauthe."
And he nikked him nay, he nolde by no wayes.
Thay acolen and kissen and kennen aither other
To the prince of Paradise, and parten right there
                    on colde;
2475   Gawain on blonk ful bene
            To the kinges burgh buskes bolde,
            And the knight in the enker grene
            Whiderwarde soever he wolde.

Wilde wayes in the worlde Wawain now rides
2480 On Gringolet, that the grace had geten of his live;
Oft he herbered in house and oft al theroute,
And mony aventure in vale, and venquist oft,
That I ne tight at this time in tale to remene.
The hurt was hole that he had hent in his nek,
2485 And the blikkande belt he bere theraboute
Abelef as a bauderik bounden by his side,
Loken under his lift arme, the lace, with a knot,
In tokening he was tan in tech of a faut.
And thus he comes to the court, knight al in sounde.
2490 There wakened wele in that wone when wist the gret
That good Gawain was comen; gain hit him thoght.
The king kisses the knight, and the quene als,
And sithen mony siker knight that soght him to hailse,
Of his fare that him frained; and ferlily he telles,
2495 Beknowes alle the costes of care that he had,
The chaunce of the chapel, the chere of the knight,

2498 *nirt:* slight cut
2499 *unleauty:* disloyalty
2501 *tened:* suffered torment
2502 *grame:* mortification
2503 *melle:* stream together
2507 *lothe:* injury
     losse: damage
2511 *bot unhap ne may hit:* without misfortune ensuing
2512 *tached:* fastened
     twinne: be separated, depart
2515 *longed:* belonged
2517 *abelef:* aslant
2518 *in sute:* in imitation, following suit
2521 *breved:* written
2522 *aunter:* adventure
2525 *sesed:* ceased
2527 *aunteres:* adventures

The luf of the lady, the lace at the last.
The nirt in the nek he naked hem shewed
That he laght for his unleauty at the leudes handes
for blame.
    He tened when he shulde telle,
    He groned for gref and grame;
    The blod in his face con melle,
    When he hit shulde shewe, for shame.

2505 "Lo, lord," quoth the leude, and the lace handeled,
"This is the bande of this blame I bere in my nek,
This is the lothe and the losse that I laght have,
Of cowardise and covetise that I have caght thare;
This is the token of untrauthe that I am tan inne,
2510 And I mot nedes hit were while I may last;
For none may hiden his harme, bot unhap ne may hit,
For there hit ones is tached, twinne wil hit never."
The king comfortes the knight, and alle the court als
Laghen loude therat, and luflily accorden
2515 That lordes and ladies that longed to the Table,
Uche burn of the brotherhede, a bauderik shulde have,
A bande abelef him aboute of a bright grene,
And that, for sake of that segg, in sute to were.
For that was accorded the renoun of the Rounde Table,
2520 And he honoured that hit had evermore after,
As hit is breved in the best boke of romaunce.
Thus in Arthures day this aunter betidde,
The Brutus bokes therof beres wittenesse;
Sithen Brutus, the bold burn, bowed hider first,
2525 After the sege and the assaut was sesed at Troye,
    iwis,
    Mony aunteres here-beforne
    Have fallen such ere this.
    Now that bere the croun of thorne,
    He bring us to his blisse.

Amen.

HONY SOYT QUI MAL PENCE

———

133

GLOSSARY

(Note: The reader is advised to learn these words, as they occur frequently in the poem.)

bede: offered
bent: open ground; battlefield or hunting field
bilive: quickly
blonk: horse
bonk: hillside, slope
bowe: go
breme: fierce, wild, brave
brenne: burn
brent: burnt
briddes: birds
bronde: sword; burnt wood
burde: lady, maiden
burgh: castle, city
burn: man, knight
busk: get ready, hasten
cach: catch, take, receive
carole: dance accompanied with song
carp: (make) conversation
cayre: ride
chere: face; expression; mood
clere: clear, bright, fair
dece: dais
der: deer
derf: bold, strong, hard, firm
dint: blow
douth: company
Drightin: God
drury: love; love-token
eft: afterwards, again
erthe: earth, ground
fange: take, get
fare: go
fele: many
felle (adj.): fierce, bold
felle (noun): skin
fer: far
ferde(n): went
ferk: go, ride, travel
firre: further

flet: floor (of hall)
folde: earth, land; *upon folde:* on earth, living
fole: horse
forthy: therefore, so
forward(es): agreement, covenant
fote: foot
frain: ask, test
fraist: ask, test, seek
fre: noble, courtly, good
freke: man, knight
fro: from
gate: way, road
geder: gather
gentile: gentle, of noble birth
gome: knight, man
graithe (verb): dress, get ready
graithe (adj.): ready
graithely: readily, promptly
greve: grove, thicket
hailse: greet
hals: neck
hathel: knight, master, lord
hem: them
hende: courteous, gracious
hent: take, catch, receive
her: their
heterly: fiercely, suddenly
highe (verb): hasten
hight: promised
hir: her
hit: it
ho: she
hode: hood
hole (adj.): whole
hom: them
hor: their
hunte: huntsman
ighe: eye
ilk: same

134

iwis: indeed, certainly
lach: seize, receive, accept
laght: past tense of *lach*
lance (verb): cut; throw, utter, fly, dash, rush
lasse: less, smaller
launde: lawn, field
lef: dear, beloved, delightful
leghten: past tense of *lach*
lel: loyal
lelly: loyally
leme: shine
lenge: stay
lenger: longer
leude: man, knight; people
leve: dear, beloved, delightful
ligges: lies
like (verb): please; *it liked him:* he liked it
list (verb): it pleases; *you list:* you wish
londe: land, ground, country
lote: sound, noise, words
luf: love
luflich: gracious, graciously
luflily: graciously
meiny: company, members of household or court.
mele: speak, say
mete (noun): food, meal
mete (verb): meet
meve: move
mo more
mony: many
moroun: morrow, morning
mot: may; must
nauther: neither, either
ne: not, nor
negh (adv.): near, nearly
negh (verb): approach
nerre: nearer
nolde: would not
of: of OR off
other: other OR or
quaint: skilful, gracious, skilfully made
quaintlich, quaintly: elegantly, daintily, skilfully

rach: hound that hunts by scent
radly: swiftly, promptly
renk: knight, man
renne: run, slide, flow
sale: hall
seche (verb): seek
segg: man, knight
segh: saw
self: self OR same
sete, seten: sat
shalk: man
shelde: shield
shire: bright, fair, white
sho: she
siker: sure, true, trusty
sithen: since, afterwards, then
sothe (adj.): true
sothe (noun): truth
stif: firm, strong, bold
stonde: stand
sturn: firm, grim, serious
swin: swine, wild boar
tan, tane: taken
tas: takes
thagh: though, even if
thair: their
thare: there
thay: they
the: the OR thee
then: then OR than
there: there OR where
thider: thither
think (verb): seems; *me think:* it seems to me
tho: those, the
thonk: thank
thurgh: through, over, because of
tide (noun): time
token: taken
trauthe: fidelity, truth, pledge
trowe: believe, think
tulk: man, knight
uche: each
wede, wedes: clothes (sometimes including armour)
welde: possess, use
wele: wealth, costliness; joy

wende (verb): turn

while: while OR until

wighe: man, knight

wlonk: noble, glorious, lovely

wone(s): dwelling, home

wone (verb): dwell, remain

yed, yeden: went

yelde: yield, repay